Central Banks and Economic Indicators
Forex Fundamental Analysis

High Impact News

DAVID CARLI

Forex News websic

x① Daily FX   - NEWSQUAWK

x② MY FX BOOK

③ INVESTING.COM

④ FXSTREET

⑤ FX FACTORY.COM

First Printing: 2017

ISBN: 9798353325147

Website: www.tradingwithdavid.com
E-mail: info@tradingwithdavid.com

EDITED

Hannah Hermes
hannahhermes@gmail.com

CONTENTS

ABOUT THE AUTHOR
INTRODUCTION

~

My journey in the investment and trading world started shortly after I graduated from the University of Pisa, Italy. I then travelled to New York City USA., where I attended exclusive courses by Steve Nison who introduced the western world to the art of the Japanese candlestick as a tool for analysing market trends and investment decisions.

I have been working as a full-time trader and an independent financial analyst since 2007 hence I established Trading with David as a niche investment service with the primary focus on FX markets and commodities. During that time, I collaborated with reputable financial trading services and investment magazines. And from 2012 -2013 I worked as a hedge fund manager for an Italian Bank boutique. In 2018, I began providing market analysis and trading ideas for a major European commodity investment company up to this date.

I published several trading and investment books to pass on my knowledge and expertise on how to analyse the financial market correctly and have the odds on your side to become a profitable trader. My approach is based on low-risk investment strategies across all markets to achieve a balanced asset allocation through diversification and risk management.

I have several other books for those who wish to learn more about certain aspects of trading such as Forex, Commodities Spread Trading, and Options so you can see how I approach other markets. Through educational channels, I coach independent investors on my personal trading strategies and how to apply them in different market conditions.

You can find out more about my educational library on https://tradingwithdavid.com to develop an extraordinary edge to your trading and investments plan with a deep understanding of the macro environment, along with advanced analysis and risk management they are designed to build or improve your trading skills.

ABOUT TRADINGVIEW

INTRODUCTION

~

My favourite trading platform is TradingView. While I have used many other platforms in the past, I have found this innovative platform has all tools and versatility that once were only reserved for investment firms' players. The popularity of this platform among active traders ranging from institutional traders, financial software companies, and retail traders is a testament to its user-friendly interface.

Created by MultiCharts as a browsing web-based charting platform. It offers a multitude of features that allow market enthusiasts to connect and collaborate via a chat window, sharing ideas and exchange opinions in real-time - this is particularly useful for those who wish to follow a certain style of trading by following specific members without the need to subscribe to their chat room at an extra cost.

Another feature that is extremely important for active traders is the ease of writing scripts. The programming language that TradingView designed is called Pine Script, it's lightweight yet powerful which lets anyone develop their own proprietary indicators and strategies to be published on the community hub.

The platform has one of the largest social networks driven by traders and investors who contribute trading ideas for the public to interact with and learn from – a place where top analysis and valuable content are presented daily by professional traders globally. With over 100 ready-to-use indicators, and over 5000 scripts commonly used for researching and backtesting. TradingView lets you discover a new world of trading and showcase your talent by being a part of a dynamic and robust community of traders.

And if speed of trade execution is your priority, TradingView allows you to integrate your account directly with your brokerage account.

Personalization is truly the greatest aspect of this platform; you could build spreads and compare two or more charts with ease. Every single instrument can be customised, and every detail can be modified. It has been my preferred charting platform for all the reasons mentioned above and more - you will be able to follow my new trading ideas and the articles that I regularly publish on TradingView to expand your knowledge and improve your trading.

PREFACE
INTRODUCTION

∼

Forex is the most exciting and dynamic market to trade. By far the largest financial market in the world with a daily volume of $6.6 trillion according to Bank of International settlement thus the most speculative market with its unique attributes that impact businesses around the world.

It is easy to start trading currencies, especially with the advent of the internet and the feasibility of opening a trading account – prompted by a plethora of Brokerage firms that require no more than a couple of hundreds of dollars to start trading currencies immediately. However, what is not easy, is being constantly profitable.

In this book, you will discover a new way of seeing the Forex market and how to analyse a currency pair. You will learn the dynamics that really move currencies and the reasons behind specific moves. We look at the forces behind the rise and fall of currency pairs – without the use of any indicators. The forex market is like an ocean, you will learn to swim with the big sharks and not be swallowed by them.

My method of trading is a culmination of over 25 years of experience in the financial markets as well as my expertise as a hedge fund manager. It is a well-defined strategy that institutional speculators use for their portfolios. By following the footsteps of the institutional traders, you will have the odds on your side. I will show you the ropes to becoming a successful forex trader.

At first glance, some concepts may seem complicated, but I assure you that with time and practice you will assimilate them without any problems, it will become second nature to apply them in your forex analysis.

You will begin to see a currency pair as a whole and not as a single entity i.e., price action – but rather as two opposing economies. A currency is the mirror of its economy; therefore, you will analyse EURUSD as the Eurozone versus the American economy. This concept is the starting point of the entire analysis that you will learn.

It took me about four years to write this book from the first edition to the latest one. As with time, new topics have been added and updated.

"*Forex with Fundamental Analysis*" is a book that will change your way of trading the forex market. With its modest price, it is my gift for all those who aspire to become professional traders.

For any questions, do not hesitate to contact me at the e-mail address info@tradingwithdavid.com it will be a pleasure to answer all of you. Also, visit my website https://tradingwithdavid.com where you will find free articles, analyses, and books.

THE HISTORY OF FOREX

CHAPTER 1

~

Forex or FX stands for "Foreign Exchange" or exchange of foreign currency, the currency purchased by travellers when visiting another country. For example, you can sell Dollars and buy Euros to travel to an EU nation (i.e., France, Portugal, or Italy). However, the online Forex market is 90% speculative, which means that the operator does not take possession of the actual currency, in physical form, but rather opens and closes trades making a profit or loss which is then recorded on the online account.

The currency market owes its existence to the abandonment of the Bretton Woods agreements in 1971 and the ensuing collapse of the fixed exchange rate regime. In 1967, a bank in Chicago refused to give a loan in Pound Sterling to a college Professor, Milton Friedman as he intended to use these funds to sell the British Pound Sterling.

Friedman had perceived that the British Pound was overvalued against the US Dollar. His intention was to sell the British Pound and then repay the bank after the Pound had depreciated, thus pocketing a quick profit. The Bank's refusal to give the loan was due to the Bretton Woods agreement which was established twenty-three years before fixing the value of the British Pound against the Dollar. The Dollar exchange rate at that time was valued at $ 45 per ounce of gold.

The Bretton Woods agreement was signed in 1944 to introduce international monetary stability to prevent the flight of capital abroad among the various nations and to restrict speculation on currencies. Before the agreement, between 1876 and the First World War, the gold trade was prevalent and dominated in the international economic system.

During this period, the currencies acquired a new phase of stability which was reinforced by the price of gold. Pegging currencies to gold was abolished since the old practices used by kings and rulers arbitrarily, devalued the money and triggered inflation. Nonetheless, the standardisation of the gold exchange had its flaws. As economies grew stronger, imports from abroad quickly increased, causing a drop in gold reserves that were needed to print money.

As a result, the money supply decreased, and interest rates levitated therefore the economic activity was reduced until recession began – this led to the prices of goods reaching rock bottom. This depreciation attracted purchases from other nations, which gave rise to a fever of purchases that were injected into the gold economy, bringing down interest rates which in turn revitalised the health of the economy.

The rapid economic expansion prevailed during this period until the First World War which interrupted the flow of trade and the free movement of goods. After the wars, the Agreement of Breton Woods was signed, and the participating countries agreed to maintain the value of their currency within a narrow margin against the US Dollar and the corresponding value of gold as needed. In various countries, it was forbidden to devalue their currency to benefit their businesses, but they were only allowed to do less than 10% devaluation in some cases.

In the 50s, the increasing expansion of trade volumes led to a massive movement of capital generated by post-war reconstruction which destabilised the exchange rates that were set in the Bretton Woods Agreement. It was finally abandoned in 1971 when the US unilaterally left the Bretton Woods agreements, and the US Dollar was no longer convertible into gold.

Since 1973, the currencies of major industrialised nations have begun to float freely, controlled mainly by supply and demand in the Forex market. The daily fluctuation of prices, the increase in sales volume and price volatility in the 70s, gave rise to new financial instruments. It was the beginning of market deregulation and liberalisation of trade.

In 1978, following the second major devaluation of the US Dollar, the fixed exchange rate mechanism was resigned entirely from the US government and replaced with a floating exchange rate. This floating exchange rate, in turn, was adopted by other major currencies, turning them into goods whose value fluctuated because of the force of supply and demand.

This free-floating exchange rate among all currencies of the world was the birth of the International foreign exchange market. In the '80s, with the advent of computers and technology, the movement of capital in the international arena has greatly accelerated – and extended to global markets throughout Asia, Europe, and the Americas.

These same technologies have made it possible for private investors to enter this market traditionally dominated only by banks and institutions. Transactions in the Forex grew from about 70 billion dollars a day in the 80s, to more than 4 trillion a day in the next three decades, with about 90% of the volumes traded for speculative purposes.

There have been several radical changes in the world economy in recent decades. Some of these changes have reduced barriers, and increased opportunities in world trade: the fall of communism in the Soviet Union and Eastern Europe, the renewed political reform in

South America and the continued liberalisation of the economy of China have launched the world economy by opening new markets and new opportunities. These events have upped their traditional trade barriers resulting in a tremendous increase in international investments.

With the increase of trade among all nations they became more interrelated and dependent on each other. It spurred international investment and paved for an expansion of economic activities to a great extent with a greater interrelationship.

Fluctuations in the economic activity of a country are reflective of the currency of that country which are immediately transferred to the commercial partners. These price changes in the products affect costs and profits therefore it affects the rate of currency exchange.

Reports of economic data releases around the world, such as inflation, unemployment levels, as well as natural disasters or political instability, decide on the convenience of owning a particular currency, and affect the international supply or demand of that currency. In general, the Forex market is vital to the prosperity of the free world economy.

Every single day currencies are bought and sold, of total value of over $6.6 trillion. It is by far the market with the most daily transactions equivalent to about four months of trading volume on the New York Stock Exchange (NYSE), which has an average daily traded value of 45 million Dollars. Forex, in essence, 100 times larger than the NYSE.

Unfortunately, from 1971 until a few years ago, the owners of this market were the major banks, brokers and the big multinational corporations, and the only way to access it, for an individual investor, was to rely on banks who demanded a minimum of one million Dollar cash deposit. Also, the sophisticated technology of communication and trading needed were not yet within the reach of most individuals.

With the great revolution of the internet, Forex online brokers allowed everyone to operate in the currency market with just a PC connected to the internet.

But what is the essence of the Forex market?

INTRODUCTION TO FOREX

CHAPTER 2

~

When trading Forex, you address scenarios that directly affect your life. For example, you purchase a product that is built outside the monetary area of residence. The final price of this product is not only affected by the production costs, but also by the evaluation of the exchange rate, which ultimately results in savings for the purchaser, equally it runs the risk of increasing costs.

One of the main influences on international trades is the exchange rates among global currencies. The FX market is unlike the stock market whereby opening and closing hours at standard times from Monday to Friday. The FX markets start trading on Sunday at 5pm starting in Asia and close on Friday at 5pm US Eastern time. This is because the currency market affects all international trade and could not be restricted to certain hours. You can see the overlap of the zones of the different financial centres that produces an increase of volatility at intersections (Figure 1).

Since the FX market is open 24 hours, in effect, it creates an additional opportunity for the development of your analysis.

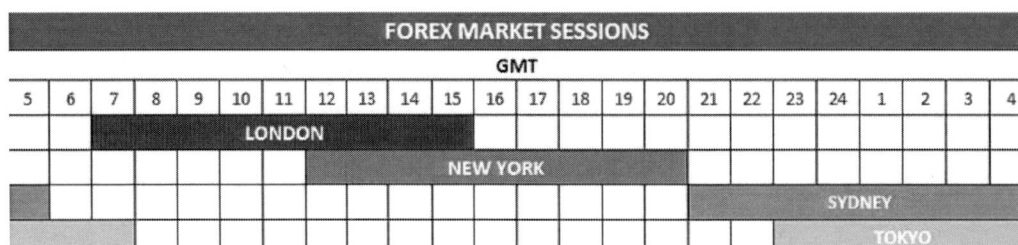

FOREX MARKET SESSIONS																								
GMT																								
5	6	7	8	9	10	11	12	13	14	15	16	17	18	19	20	21	22	23	24	1	2	3	4
		LONDON																					
							NEW YORK																
																SYDNEY							
																			TOKYO				

Figure 1 - The Forex Market Sessions (GMT)

As you can see, the largest and most interesting overlap occurs between the London session, as it's considered the most important FX session in Europe, and the New York session. During this period, the volatility increases dramatically due to many operators that influence the supply and demand of various currencies. So, the probability of having high volatility during the overlap of the two financial centres (London and New York) is very high.

Other overlaps are Sydney and Tokyo, and between Tokyo and London.

The absence of a centralised headquarters in Forex with its predefined times of daily opening and closing makes it over the counter market often referred to as OTC. Trading takes place directly between two parties without going through the exchange, therefore, you can easily access the online virtual market anywhere in the world.

As mentioned in the previous chapter, the Forex market is the largest and most liquid in the world, with over $6.6 trillion in daily trading. Trades are 90% speculative, generated not only by the large investors and investment banks but also by private investors with small capital through leverage.

For example, if you invest with a leverage ratio of 1:100, this means for every $1 you're trading, you can trade up to $100 capital. The leverage, then, is a double-edged sword because your profits increase but also your losses are multiplied compared to your real investment. It is a reward that the market offers, but only if you use it well to benefit from this incentive.

Another important aspect regarding Forex is that it is bi-directional, that is, you can get profit in both directions – when the market goes up or down.

In the Forex market, you are going to buy and sell a currency compared with another one (currency pair). So, when you buy a currency pair, you buy the base currency (the first), and you sell the quote currency (the second). When you sell a currency pair, you sell the base currency, and you buy the quote currency.

For example, if you decide to sell USDCAD, all you need to do is sell US Dollars which also means you bought the Canadian Dollars. If you buy EURJPY, you are purchasing Euros and selling Japanese Yen.

To close the trade that you have opened, you must do the opposite of the previous trade. If, for example, you bought Euro and sold British pounds but now you want to close the trade, therefore you should buy an equal amount of the British Pound and sell Euro in order to have a zero net position. This can be done directly from the trading platform when you give the order to close the trade.

In the Forex market, there are eight major currencies that makeup 80% of trade. Seven of these currencies, coupled with the eighth, the US Dollar (USD), form the so-called "Majors." They are:

EURUSD, USDCHF, GPBUSD, USDJPY, USDCAD, AUDUSD, NZDUSD.

Currency pairs that do not contain the US Dollar are known as Cross-Currency Pairs or only "Crosses." Historically, if you wanted to convert a currency, you would first have to convert the currency into US Dollars and then into the currency which you desired.

With the introduction of the Crosses, you no longer have to do this tedious calculation as all brokers now offer direct exchange rates. The most active crosses are derived from the three major non-US Dollar currencies (Euro, UK British Pound, and Japanese Yen). These currency pairs are also known as "Minors." An example:

EURJPY, EURGBP, EURCHF, AUDNZD, NZDJPY, GBPJPY, AUDJPY, GBPCAD etc.

We also have what is called "Exotics" which are made up of a major currency paired with one of an emerging market or a strong but smaller economy from a global perspective, such as Singapore, South Africa, or European countries outside of the Eurozone.

These currency pairs are not traded as often as the majors or crosses, so the cost of trading with these currency pairs can be higher, due to the lack of liquidity in these markets.

An example: USDSGD, EURSEK, USDRUB, EURTRY, USDZAR, EURDKK, USDNOK, USDMXN etc.

The major players in the Forex market are the Central Banks, investment banks, institutional investors, and hedge funds which, thanks to their financial capabilities, move the entire market. Along with that, we have seen private investors (retail traders) participating as well. They are, however, a tiny part, from the point of view of the capital held, compared to the big banks or hedge funds.

Precisely because these retail investors are so small, they become prey for the big speculators with the possibility of being hunted. Most novice traders without any experience suffer huge losses because they are focused on the wrong things within the market. So, they make errors due to a lack of experience, such as the wrong position size.

But how do you progress from being a hunted prey to a trader that follows what large investors do? thus becoming profitable over time? At the start of my trading career, I tried many strategies, but most of them had limitations in practice. They were based on tools (indicators) that essentially derived from a mathematical calculation – they were unable to evaluate the constant development of the market. I too was dealing with evolving markets (Forex, equities, commodity, etc.) using the same restricted tools.

An example of this would be if a person dressed all year round in the same clothes without considering the change of seasons from colder to warmer days. The same is true in the Forex market and in trading in general. How would an indicator address these situations? It would always be an identical result because it is based on unchanging statistical and mathematical calculations. So, it may not be the most appropriate method for all situations that arise when you operate in the markets.

How can you approach this market then and be profitable, having at least the statistics on your side? possible if you understand some important benchmarks - I am talking about the Central Banks (which you will see in the next chapters), it is the real market makers in Forex which move the value of each individual economy in a realistic way (not speculative).

Whenever Central banks' meetings take place, they capture the attention of the major players, and the release of economic data is a mirror of the true state of each individual economy. They provide essential information and fundamental boundaries to distinguish what is the real strength of the individual currency from what is speculative.

These considerations are based on the method that you will see explained later, which allows me to manage my portfolio. Not only with the currencies but also with other instruments linked to the Forex market (such as options). It is crucial to have definite detailed plans and always know how to behave in every situation without falling prey to emotions which are often bad counsellors.

TECHNICAL ANALYSIS VS FUNDAMENTAL ANALYSIS

CHAPTER 3

∼

Fundamental analysis and technical analysis represent two different approaches that can be made when you trade Forex and other instruments. The first has to do with the so-called fundamentals of the economy and its economic aspects. While the second focuses particularly on the price movements of a currency pair to understand and predict its subsequent movements.

Both fundamental and technical analysis are useful in Forex: the two approaches can also be used together, for analysing financial market trends satisfactorily and profitably.

Technical Analysis

Technical analysis is the study of price trends with the use of charts. The interest of a technical analyst is to look for graphic representations that are drawn by price movements. Technical analysts evaluate market trends to understand possible future price movements.

Conventional technical analysis is not based on any fundamentals of the underlying asset but rather applies a series of technical tools drawn on the chart, to allow for anticipation of future price movements.

The tools available to a trader who wants to achieve this goal are many: among these, you have trading indicators, which are specific mathematical formulas that are heuristic or pattern-based signals produced by the price or other variables. A technical analyst can look at the charts, in the short-term, medium-term, or long-term and decide whether a currency pair is destined to fall or rise.

The primary objective of indicators used by technical analysts is to try and predict the next price movements. One of the most overused indicators is the "simple moving average", which is calculated on a certain amount of price data and is constantly updated as it moves from period to period. Given an average of a certain time frame, the most recent data is added each time, eliminating the last data in the series from the calculation.

The moving average can be used as a watershed between bullish and bearish trends, or as dynamic support or resistance (a concept that we will explore further on in this book).

Fundamental Analysis

When we talk about fundamental analysis, we refer to the process of breaking down the impact of macroeconomic and social factors on the relative value of the currency. The part of the economy that has to do with the forecasts on fundamental drivers.

In fact, the price development of a currency pair also depends on geopolitical events, economic crises, wars, acquisitions of companies and multinationals, central bank meetings, market rumours, and so on. Based on this approach, therefore, traders can understand and analyse the economic aspects that are dependent on price development and then exploit them to profit from such news.

The main difference between fundamental analysis and technical analysis is that for a fundamental analyst, it is necessary to examine balance sheets, data releases and statistics, whilst the second refers essentially to the study of the charts.

Hence, a fundamental analyst focuses on economic theory and related accounting, econometric and statistical methods: it is an approach that, as you can guess, is based on a longer period compared to the horizon of technical analysis.

The technical analysis can be set to different timeframes, a few minutes or even years. Whereas fundamental analysis does not have the same freedom of choice, as the data must be interpreted over time. Fundamental analysis and technical analysis, in essence, are concepts with a conflicting application of Forex, but it does not mean that they cannot coexist; in fact, several traders combine them in their analyses.

For example, the tools of technical analysis can be useful to a fundamental analyst to give him the opportunity to understand when the most suitable time for the market entry (the timing) is. On the other hand, a technical analyst can decide which indicators to use as technical signals in addition to the economic fundamentals. In a nutshell, the buy or sell decision comes from a pattern on a chart that is also supported by fundamental data.

Crucially, we must understand the differences and the characteristics of the two types of analysis. Starting from the importance of timing: this element, which is very significant for a successful trader, can be understood as the best time for market entry. With the right timing, the stop-loss is closer, which means higher odds of success and a reduction in losses.

The study of the charts (i.e., the technical analysis) allows you to understand the key levels of the timing. Another factor that deserves to be taken into consideration is that, sometimes, an event can already be priced into the market sentiment or price. In essence, fundamental analysis is incorporated into technical analysis. In other words, within the charts, prices are reflective of all the elements of fundamental analysis (the ones we mentioned earlier; political events, economic crises, and so on).

Furthermore, it is worth pointing out that the fundamental analysis is less flexible than technical analysis, which allows one to focus on stop-losses and above all, to program the various objectives for other timeframes.

Lastly, the aspect of finding information with ease. At one point, finding news and data was very complicated, especially for an average investor. Nowadays, thanks to the rise of internet search engines, anyone can find all the data and news to carry out a complete analysis. And that is what you will see later.

In any case, you must not make the mistake of believing that for a long-term investment, you must opt for fundamental analysis, while for a short-term investment, you choose technical analysis. A watertight compartments division of this type of analysis is neither fruitful nor correct. With the appropriate measures and adequate knowledge, both methods can be useful in the short, medium, and long term.

So, which of the two methods to use? Maybe a combination of both?

When I worked for an Italian investment bank for two years, managing as a fund manager, I have seen enough evidence to conclude that technical analysis is not a source of alpha or edge.

In an investment bank, nobody uses technical analysis. No indicator or oscillator is used, not even Fibonacci, Gann, or Elliott. The only thing traders of an investment bank looked at was the fundamentals. The only way to earn in trading is to increase your skills. No system makes you earn money automatically otherwise, do not you think the big investment banks would have used these indicators instead of employing hundreds of traders to assess the big macro picture?

When you trade, it is necessary to study the reasons that drive the prices, and what moves them – you must learn the fundamental logic and not trade by looking at the charts only.

And this is what you will learn in this book: to trade currencies like an investment bank.

INSIDE A CURRENCY PAIR

CHAPTER 4

When we look at a currency pair, for example, EURUSD, we mustn't see it as a single market, or as one price action – it's incorrect. Instead, we need to see it in a completely different way. We must go behind the scenes and understand the dynamics and how the currency pair is formed. By doing this, we will understand the mechanics behind it so that we use it to our advantage when trading the pair.

Again, we ought to see the currency pair as two variables separately, much the same as spread trading. When trading EURUSD, we analyse two separate economies: the Eurozone economy versus the US economy and not as a single market. By doing so, we examine each economy singly - this process will allow us to find strengths and weaknesses in each economy which then, these tendencies will materialise and develop with time.

Conversely, when trading stocks, let's take Facebook, for example, we look at the chart and its price movements, we know one of the fundamentals of the company is earnings – and if Facebook releases earnings lower than expected, the stock is expected to fall even though the Nasdaq index might rise considerably. Which peg the question, could we trade the EURUSD and treat it the same as Facebook? here we have a currency pair that constitutes two economies - clearly not. You cannot treat an individual company as two combined economies. All I am saying is that you should be acutely aware of the differences, and this is what I am going to delve into.

Learning Forex is essential for all markets even if you do not trade forex. Whatever market do you decide to trade be it commodities, spread trading, or options (mainly in the US market)? We are dealing with transactions that require currencies in every country – profits and losses are measured in their functional currencies - be it Dollars, Euros, Canadian Dollars, or the Australian Dollar, and so forth. Hence, learning the Forex driving forces for managing foreign exchange risks will be very advantageous to your trading.

Often, you hear about correlations (more about this later). Within Forex, the correlation between an economy and a commodity is interesting because the price of raw materials may heavily influence an economy and you will understand the concept better when

15

we get to Chapter 20 "Commodity Currencies".

One aspect you are going to see that I find important is the "Safe-Haven Currencies". When we speak of safe-haven assets, we refer to gold and silver, in forex you can hedge your portfolio, with currencies such as the Swiss Franc and the Japanese Yen.

We will explore safe-haven currencies in more depth in Chapter 19. As you trade currencies, it is crucial to always remember that this market was created primarily for international trade.

Be cognisant that within the currency market, there are sub-factors that play a major role, such as speculative operations that come with enormous leverage. Leverage is nothing but a "game" invented to persuade more people to enter the market – to fathom this concept of leverage, ask yourself, would Apple lure its customers to buy an iPhone for $20 with leverage? Try going to the Apple Store and purchasing an iPhone for $ 20 tempted with leverage.

Those of you that worked with high leverage got to see what happened at the beginning of 2015 with the Swiss Franc, and how much you can really lose with this "little game." Very often Forex is seen as lucrative with the leverage notion in mind. Leverage is a risky game that has been offered by brokers with a double-edged sword – but what exactly leverage is? Leverage means you're only required to put up a small amount of money (known as margin) to control a much larger amount. It enables retail traders to open positions without locking away a huge amount worth of capital. However, it magnifies both your profits and your losses.

This is what often happens in the Forex market, and that is why so many people lose a lot of money trading Forex, perhaps even more than in any other market. The reality is, if trading Forex is handled the right way, you will be able to handle the risks associated with it adequately, thus becoming a good market for you to exploit.

CENTRAL BANKS

CHAPTER 5

~

As I previously mentioned, the biggest market maker that moves the currency market is the Central bank.

A central bank is a national institution that manages the currency of a country or group of countries and controls the money supply, literally, the amount of money in circulation. The main objective of many central banks is price stability. In some countries, central banks are also required by law to act in support of full employment.

One of the main tools of a central bank is setting interest rates, the "cost of money", as part of its monetary policy. The central bank is not a commercial bank. An individual cannot open an account in a central bank or ask for a loan, as with a public bank, it is not motivated by profit. Central banks have the power and decide whether to cut or raise interest rates, they build money creation programs, and adopt policies to extend or narrow the value of the individual economies and, consequently, the weight of their currencies. Their decisions can drastically move the foundations of an economy and, above all, can influence project development in the following months.

If supply and demand are the underlying logic that moves a currency pair – what moves the markets, then? Markets are not moved by central banks (they are market makers) and most certainly technical analysis patterns or indicators in the overbought or oversold zone don't move the market. These moves are initiated by investment banks that hold favourable advantageousness on their side. With their large positions in the market, they can tip the balance of supply and demand of currencies traded per se.

Their investment models are derived from Central Banks' directives; whereby large institutional investors take their trading decisions. And that is the logic behind trading or investing in the medium to long-term is purely based on the thoughts of those who move these currencies and the economies.

Accordingly, you can take advantage of these situations exactly as the big investors do.

Figure 2 - EURUSD weekly chart (TradingView.com)

Let us look at an example to gain a better understanding of this. In Figure 2 above, you can see the EURUSD weekly chart. On January 22, 2015, at the ECB meeting, it was announced the asset purchase program, the QE (Quantitative Easing). Namely, the Euro currency injection in the market.

The announcement of the QE program introduction caused a drop of EURUSD from about 1.1600 to a price that has come to hit 1.1115 in less than 24 hours.

By using several conventional indicators, many traders (I personally know some of them) saw an opportunity to enter a bullish position, after the first bearish wave on January 22, the large investors capitalised on this move and pushed the currency pair further down on January 23 - negating all strategies that traders tend to use, which are essentially visual analyses that are limited by static indicators and fundamentally unsupported of economic trends.

Forex and other markets, in general, not only have technical levels but also fundamental levels. In the chart the level of 1.1600, as you have seen, is the value of EURUSD when Mario Draghi announced the Quantitative Easing (QE), where it was formed as a "fundamental resistance." above that level would invalidate the macroeconomic environment created by the ECB.

Important! Keep in mind that in the markets as in life, everything is possible. I am not saying it is impossible to exceed 1.1600, because if in the medium to long-term central banks move the currencies, the short- time enables speculation to do it. However, it is a significant level, and therefore not easy to overcome. This will be the case until conditions change.

So, when we go to think about building large positions against the market makers, we must consider the idea of putting ourselves in opposition to someone much stronger and bigger than us.

It is important to understand what moves you should make to gain a statistical advantage resulting from those who hold power (central banks), compared to the indicators and everything in the trading world landscape.

Now, to conclude this chapter, let's see who the main Central Banks are.

- United States: **Federal Reserve (Fed)**
- Canada: **Bank of Canada (BoC)**
- Eurozone: **European Central Bank (ECB)**
- Great Britain: **Bank of England (BoE)**
- Switzerland: **Swiss National Bank (SNB)**
- Japan: **Bank of Japan (BoJ)**
- Australia: **Reserve Bank of Australia (RBA)**
- New Zealand: **Reserve Bank of New Zealand (RBNZ)**
- China: **People's Bank of China (PBoC)**

These are all the real market makers in the financial markets in general. On their sites, you can find and read the reports and minutes of various meetings.

They are very important in building and revising your operational plans. By creating the thesis of a possible outcome for each currency, you can get a complete macroeconomic overview that can help you in many situations.

Constructing a comprehensive plan with the most important news and macroeconomic data is also the method used by traders who work in investment banks. Why? Because, as I mentioned, they do not rely on any indicator that is in the overbought or oversold zone, but rather align themselves with where the sharks are, and the largest sharks are the central banks, they hold the most capital. They are the ones who run the entire economy, and everyone follows their steps - most certainly you don't want to be on the wrong side.

One comment from them, good or bad, can create a strong movement in the market, and as we know the world of currencies affects directly or indirectly the rest of the financial markets. Understanding currencies becomes crucial to avoiding unpleasant situations in other markets. For example, commodities are traded in US Dollars, and therefore, the value of the Dollar tends to influence them (e.g., a Dollar too strong is negative for the commodities).

Important! safe to say, sometimes a decision is announced days or weeks before the central bank meeting is held. So, often, the decisions have already been priced into the market.

LONG-TERM TRADING

CHAPTER 6

~

To understand this type of trading, you must start with the concept of trading with a long-term goal, where planning has the capacity to remain implicit for several months, but with time the real values of the economies come to fruition according to the original analysis that we set out after the central bank announcement or other related news.

I practically do not use technical analysis. I only consider the static supports and resistances given by volumes when I decide on the market entry. In my trading, in the management of my money, I have always tried to reproduce, as far as I could, the same work when I was a fund manager simply because investment banks only use fundamental analysis that has more weight in the med-long term and that is my style of trading.

Figure 3 - EURUSD weekly chart (TradingView.com)

The first step, which must become a habitual procedure, is to subdivide the legs that form the currency pair. Remember, currency pairs are relational. You must analyse each leg (each currency, i.e., each economy), and then exploit the strengths of one and the weaknesses of the other. *Think like the Central Banks*

By the same token, who determines the value of a company? It's the chair of the company. And who is the chair of the "Dollar" company? It's the Fed. Equally, the chair of the Euro company is the ECB. Therefore, each central bank controls its own currency. Once you recognise a currency as a representative of a company; and see it from this perspective, it becomes clearer that the Dollar is a company with its Chair, Jerome Powell.

In this broader context, we approach the currency pair by enlisting the pros and cons of each economy and defining the strengths and weaknesses of both.

Let's return to the example of EURUSD of the previous chapter (Figure 3 above) and implement these steps. We begin by building summaries from (February 2017) of the current state of the different economies, we look for strengths that could boost the currency, or weaknesses that would affect it, in a very negative way.

Let's start with <u>Euros</u>.

- Brexit
- Immigration
- Security (terrorist attacks in France, Belgium, Germany)
- Political Elections in Germany, France, and the Netherlands
- Extending QE = Injection of currency by the ECB
- Different economies inside
- Low Inflation

<u>Much liquidity = Devaluation of the currency (Euro)</u>

We conclude that the European Union has the characteristics of an economy with increased liquidity in circulation and with serious structural problems.

Upon identifying these points regarding the Euro, we examine the European Union (27 countries) to find out any issues that may hinder our final assessment. And we apply the same approach with regards to the US Dollar i.e., we build all the pros and cons, including future external factors that may influence the US Dollar.

- Domestic consumption-based economy
- Currency used for international trade
- Good jobs data
- Economy growing at a faster rate
- Three projected rate increase in 2017
- Political uncertainty caused by Donald Trump

22

- Problems with the budget deficit

<u>Rate increase = Even stronger Dollar</u>

The economy grows at a faster pace, but also must deal with the Trump policy and a very strong Dollar, hence damaging exports.

So, on one hand, you have the Euro economy still weak and with various problems and uncertainties. On the other hand, the US economy is booming with the Fed ready to raise interest rates three times in 2017, a move that most certainly is a manoeuvre for absorbing the huge injection of QE liquidity.

Now, in order to develop these possible arguments for each economy, you need to start from ground up, identifying the core characteristics of each currency of that economy based on real data and not from an assumption or hearsay based on news, social media, or rumours – so that your analysis is tangible and logical from a real standpoint, once you have a clear understanding of both economies only then you will be able to trade that currency pair.

In summary, you must build these scenarios and create your trading probability model with practical levels, where you can take advantage of market situations. The analysis will lead you to a clear, definite and, most of all, concrete trading plan, where you will not suffer emotionally, and most of all, you will not be chewed by the big sharks.

In the next chapter, we cover economic indicators to help you understand and evaluate primary data and how to properly analyse a currency pair.

MACROECONOMICS

CHAPTER 7

~

While macroeconomics is at the heart of the decision to buy and sell currencies, it is far beyond the scope of this chapter to explain the vast theories. What's more, it would be arrogant to pretend that this chapter will cover all the macroeconomic principles as well as not the objective of this book. I will only give an introduction, and some notions, so that you have a clearer understanding of the concepts and data that influence the currency market and to easily decipher the following chapters.

Macroeconomics is the study of aggregate economic relations between all economic agents - consumers, enterprises, and the state. In particular, the causes of economic growth, expansion, recession cycles, and the effects they have on employment and prices.

Thus, there are three main economic factors that are considered by macroeconomics:

- GDP-Gross Domestic Product (the growth rate)
- unemployment rate
- Inflation (the change in prices)

The task of macroeconomics is to identify the equilibrium values between these three components. Typically, an economy grows at a certain 'potential' rate, which is associated with a stable unemployment rate and inflation.

Macroeconomics also examines the links between the three factors mentioned above. For example, if the GDP (growth rate) is particularly positive, we will see a fall in unemployment which will lead to an increase in inflation, causing the initial equilibrium state to be lost.

Macroeconomics, therefore, investigates the loss of equilibrium that occurs and examines how the effects impact production (labour and capital) and prices (wages and interest rate).

GDP, Gross Domestic Product, is defined as "the value of all final goods and services produced within a country in a specified period". The GDP, thereby, is a monetary measure of the value of all final goods and services provided in the unit of time considered, which generally corresponds to one year.

GDP does not include:

- Intermediate goods, that is goods derived from the processing of other goods. Let me give you an example: in the production of bread, the wheat used (raw material) must be considered, but the value of the flour used (materials derived from the processing of wheat), is subtracted from the value of the wheat that has already been counted in the GDP. Simply put, we are only concerned with the exact value of the actual wheat excluding any materials added or costs associated with the final product. This process calculates the exact usage of unit - that are added to the GDP, known in economics as "value-added".

- the values from the sale of already existing assets. The sale of a house for example, that already exists, is not included in the GDP calculation, because it is not part of the current production. It only includes the services provided to sell it, such as the commissions paid to the real estate agent. Only if a house is newly built, then it is taken into account when determining GDP.

However, GDP also includes depreciation, i.e., the depreciation of all equipment (including non-physical equipment such as computer software) that goes to make up the production system, which loses value over time as "wear and tear" and therefore needs to be continually restored.

There are three methods for calculating the value of GDP, depending on the point of view from which the approach is taken.

- Expenditure Method: examines GDP from the demand side (from the point of view of the person who buys and pays a price for the product/service). It is therefore quite intuitive to understand that the GDP is composed of consumption such as household spending on durable goods, consumer goods and services, investments (business and household spending on capital goods and real estate), government spending (state and government spending) and net exports (the difference between exports and imports).

- Value added method: examines the GDP from the side of those who sell the product or service (i.e., the supply side). In order to get to the final point of the production process, (the sale) a series of operations are carried out such as the purchase of intermediate goods-raw materials, semi-finished products and productive factors-labour and capital goods, which allow each step to add value: adding up all the added values of the productive step we arrive at the same value of GDP obtained with the previous method.

- Income method: examines the problem from another point of view, namely that factors of production contributed to final goods – which are essentially labour and financial capital employed. These factors must be remunerated (income earned) including wages and profits – to some there are taxes to be added on services and VAT (a kind of remuneration for the state for the services it provides), all of which constitute a net of production subsidies.

Gross Domestic Product is the main indicator of the health of an economic system, as it represents the system's ability to produce and sell goods. Analyses of past and present GDP trends and estimates of future developments are the focus of analysts and economists. The GDP is the most important variable in economic policy decisions as consistent and constant growth rates guarantee high levels of prosperity and tax revenues that can support public budgets.

The inflation rate measures the general increase in prices and is a key variable in macroeconomics. Not only economists watch at this Figure with concern but also governments and ordinary people as it is an indicative of health of the economy.

This concern would have no meaning if the increase in inflation affected everything (including wages and pensions) in the same percentage. In that case, we would be talking about "pure inflation". Instead, prices rise in different proportions, influencing and changing not only consumer choices (especially those of the middle class) but also those regarding investments and production.

Rising inflation generates worry and uncertainty, reducing confidence in the economy and being reflected negatively in the markets. This is due to a demand shock (if it becomes much higher than supply) or a supply shock (increase in production costs, typical of raw materials) and causes changes in production rate and income.

Very high inflation (25%-30% per month or more) is called *hyperinflation*. With hyperinflation, prices are subject to uncontrollable increases that are so high that they are measured on a monthly basis or even on a shorter time reference.

Without mentioning such extreme cases from the past (such as Germany in 1922/24) an example can be seen in Venezuela, whose inflation was at the time of writing this chapter, over 3,000% per year, the highest in the world.

The excess of money supply that creates hyperinflation is due to the state's need to finance public spending through the central bank by creating money because it is unable, or unwilling, to do so through taxes or debt.

The central banks' concern is *stagflation* (a combination of terms stagnation and inflation), which indicates a situation in which there is both a general increase in prices (inflation) and a lack of growth in the economy in real terms (economic stagnation) with high levels of unemployment.

The economic slowdown means less work while higher prices erode the purchasing power of households forced to pay more for bills, fuel and food leaving less room for other consumption.

Employment, more specifically the unemployment rate, is another crucial aspect of a country's economy. A couple of simple formulas. The labour force is obtained by adding the employed people to the unemployed:

Labour force = people employed + unemployed

The unemployment rate, on the other hand, is the number of unemployed divided by the labour force:

Unemployment rate = unemployed persons/labour force

However, there are different interpretations of unemployment depending on the country which can lead to confusion. There are countries where, after a certain amount of time, a person without a job no longer falls into the category of "unemployed" but is considered "idle", i.e., a person who has no intention of finding employment.

In addition to the three mentioned above, there are several other macroeconomic data that are useful to analyse the various aspects of a country's economy and which you will see listed in the next chapter.

Based on the values of the main macroeconomic data, the state adopts economic policy measures to counteract adverse economic conditions, promote economic growth, create, and spread social consensus, reduce unemployment and more generally, steer the economy of a country. Economic plans are complex, and they take into account all the possible implications of each strategy.

Each economic policy intervention is developed through the adoption of both monetary and fiscal policy measures. In fact, the amount of money present in an economic system influences the interest rate and income. This approach is determined autonomously by the monetary authorities, that is the central banks.

In the short-term, monetary policy can influence economic growth. For example, a reduction in the interest rate, which you will see later usually leads to a devaluation of the exchange rate, hence stimulating investment and exports.

The primary objective of monetary policy implemented by central banks is price stability (i.e., inflation) in the medium-term. This means that it is possible to have periods of higher or lower inflation in the short term. Therefore, there are no constraints on the amount of money that can be injected into the economy, hence the inflation that can be generated.

Variations in the quantity of money circulating in a country are obtained through so-called "open market operations". In particular:

a) if a central bank intends to reduce the quantity of money in the system, it proceeds to sell securities in exchange for money. In this way, it removes part of the money present on the market (deflation).

b) If a central bank wants to increase the amount of money in the system, it buys securities in exchange for money. In this way, it introduces additional quantities of money into the system.

Therefore, the presence of money, in its multiple functions influences the behaviour of the economic operators, above all through the variations of the interest rate. Overall, money is divided into:

- **M1**, the circulating money composed of banknotes, coins, and current account deposits
- **M2**, includes, in addition to M1, short-term deposits, i.e., with a maturity of fewer than 2 years, and those redeemable on demand within 3 months
- **M3**, which includes M1 and M2 and adds other forms of negotiable liabilities such as investment fund shares, repos, and bonds with a maturity of fewer than two years

The central bank has an instrument at its disposal which is the interest rate and a target to pursue the inflation rate. The mechanism is based on two components: the influence of monetary policy on the term structure of interest rates and the effect of the interest rate on investment and prices. It can be applied quickly and effectively; the interest rate is the price of money that influences the choices of both households and investors.

Depending on the rate, households can decide whether to keep their income in their current account (for spending, consumption, or as a precaution to protect themselves against the unexpected) or to buy, for example, government bonds in exchange for interest. So, the higher the interest rate, the more they will be tempted to buy government bonds.

Companies too rely on the interest rate to determine how much investment to make. If they do not have enough equity capital or if it is insufficient to implement the entire program, they need to decide whether to scale down investments or borrow capital. In the latter case, companies will issue securities (bonds) on which they will pay interest.

The interest rate acts as the mechanism for matching savings and investment, and the state will have to consider its policies – they are determined by the monetary authority which is the central bank. To set the level of the interest rate variable in search of macroeconomics equilibrium, the interest rate must be appropriate and well-thought-out.

We could also see economic policy development through the adoption of fiscal policy measures which can be detected in two ways: by the increase or decrease of public expenditure and taxes.

Fiscal policy changes income directly and acts indirectly on the demand for money through interest rate, then creates an extended impact on income ergo investment.

An economic policy consisting of a combination of fiscal policy and monetary policy that reduces the *crowding-out* effect of government spending is called "accommodative". Displacement is the mechanism whereby an increase in public spending leads to a reduction in private investment. Thus, the crowding-out effect reduces private spending on both consumption and investment.

Expansionary fiscal policy produces a reduction in private investment. The increase in public spending generates a situation of excess demand for money in the money market, which forces operators to sell securities in order to obtain liquidity. The sale of securities depresses their price by increasing the interest rate, which ultimately reduces (crowds out) investment spending in aggregate demand.

Macroeconomics is much broader and deeper than that. In this short chapter, I hope I gave you an overview to better understand some of the concepts which are used in the rest of the book. Of course, macroeconomics is certainly an interesting topic and for those who wish to explore it, and study it in-depth, there are many books to choose from to give it the attention it deserves. However, it is not the intention of this book, except for how it relates to the forex market.

The aim here is to understand the macroeconomic data and its role in the monetary policy of a central bank to establish the correct value of a currency pair and how to use it to your advantage whilst trading.

MACROECONOMIC DATA

CHAPTER 8

~

Jobs and unemployment, GDP, consumption, and inflation. These are the fields you must concentrate on when you want to get a clear and unfiltered picture of an economy.

This is because, when you read a piece of news, the author always includes, sometimes subconsciously, their own bias, thus even without intending to, you get more of an opinion than a fact or reality.

Every day, Forex traders (as well as others) study and analyse news and macroeconomic data to exploit it for profit in their trading activities. When news comes out, it creates a slight instability in currency, this currency tends to gain or lose purchasing power, that is, to gain or lose value against other currencies.

It is noteworthy that it is not necessary to be an expert economist, all you need to do is to dedicate yourself to trading, just as you would for any other job, with dedication and professionalism trading can be a source of income or supplementary to your existing job.

Let's see what the major and most important economic indicators are for the nine leading economies.

UNITED STATES

Non-Farm Payrolls: Change in the number of employed people during the previous month, excluding the farming industry. Job creation is an important leading indicator of consumer spending, which accounts for most of the overall economic activity. This is vital economic data normally released shortly after the month ends. The combination of importance and weight has a hefty impact on the markets – released monthly usually on the first Friday after the month ends.

Unemployment Rate: Percentage of the total workforce that is unemployed and actively seeking employment during the previous month. Although it is generally viewed as a lagging indicator, the number of unemployed people is an important signal of overall economic health because consumer spending is highly correlated with labour-market conditions –

released monthly usually on the first Friday after the month ends.

Average Hourly Earnings: Change in the price businesses pays for labour, excluding the farming industry. It is a leading indicator of consumer inflation - when businesses pay more for labour, the higher costs are usually passed on to the consumer – released monthly usually on the first Friday after the month ends.

GDP q/q: Annualised change in the inflation-adjusted value of all goods and services produced by the economy. Gross Domestic Product (GDP) is the broadest measure of economic activity and the primary gauge of the economy's health. There are three versions of GDP:

- Advance GDP q/q: It is the earliest and thus tends to have the most impact. Released quarterly, about 30 days after the quarter ends.
- Prelim GDP q/q: Released quarterly, about 60 days after the quarter ends.
- Final GDP q/q: Released quarterly, about 85 days after the quarter ends.

ISM Manufacturing PMI: Level of a diffusion index based on surveyed purchasing managers, excluding the manufacturing industry. A Survey of about 400 purchasing managers asks respondents to rate the relative level of business conditions including employment, production, new orders, prices, supplier deliveries, and inventories. It is a leading indicator of economic health when businesses react quickly to market conditions, with purchasing managers holding perhaps the most current and relevant insight into the company's view of the economy – released monthly on the third business day after the month ends.

CPI m/m: Change in the price of goods and services purchased by consumers. CORE version: change in the price of goods and services purchased by consumers, excluding food and energy. Consumer prices account for most of the overall inflation.

Inflation: This is important to currency valuation because rising prices lead the central bank to raise interest rates out of respect for their inflation containment mandate – released monthly about 16 days after the month ends.

PPI m/m: Change in the price of finished goods and services sold by producers. The Producer Price Index (PPI) is a leading indicator of consumer inflation. When manufacturers pay more for goods, the higher costs are usually passed on to the consumer – released monthly about 14 days after the month ends.

Retail Sales: Change in the total value of sales at the retail level. It is the primary gauge of consumer spending, which accounts for most of the overall economic activity – released monthly about 13 days after the month ends.

Building Permits: Annualised number of new residential building permits issued during the previous month. It is an excellent gauge of future construction activity because obtaining a permit is among the first steps in constructing a new building – released monthly about 17 days after the month ends.

Existing Home Sales: Annualised number of residential buildings that were sold during the previous month, excluding new construction. It is a leading indicator of economic health because the sale of a home triggers a wide-reaching ripple effect. For example, renovations are done by the new owners, a mortgage is sold by the financing bank, and brokers are paid to execute the transaction – released monthly about 20 days after the month ends.

CANADA

Unemployment Rate: Percentage of the total workforce that is unemployed and actively seeking employment during the previous month. Although it is generally viewed as a lagging indicator, the number of unemployed people is an important signal of overall economic health because consumer spending is highly correlated with labour-market conditions – released monthly about 8 days after the month ends.

GDP m/m: Change in the inflation-adjusted value of all goods and services produced by the economy. It is the broadest measure of economic activity and the primary gauge of the economy's health. Canada is unique in that they release fresh GDP data monthly. A quarterly GDP figure is also released; however, it is merely a summation of the monthly data – released monthly about 60 days after the month ends.

CPI m/m: Change in the price of goods and services purchased by consumers. That is the most important inflation-related release due to its early and broad scope. Consumer prices account for most of the overall inflation. Inflation is important to currency valuation because rising prices lead the central bank to raise interest rates out of respect for their inflation containment mandate – released monthly about 20 days after the month ends.

Manufacturing Sales m/m: Change in the total value of sales made by manufacturers. It is a leading indicator of economic health - manufacturers are quickly affected by market conditions and changes in their sales can be an early signal of future activity such as spending, hiring, and investment – released monthly about 45 days after the month ends.

Core Retail Sales: Change in the total value of sales at the retail level, excluding automobiles. Automobile sales account for about 20% of Retail Sales, but they tend to be very volatile and distort the underlying trend. The core data is, therefore, thought to be a better gauge of spending trends – released monthly about 50 days after the month ends.

Trade Balance: Difference in value between imported and exported goods during the reported month. Export demand and currency demand are directly linked because foreigners must buy the domestic currency to pay for the nation's exports.

Export demand also impacts the production and prices of domestic manufacturers. A positive number indicates that more goods were exported than imported – released monthly about 35 days after the month ends.

EUROZONE

Unemployment Rate: Percentage of the total workforce that is unemployed and actively seeking employment during the previous month. Although it is generally viewed as a lagging indicator, the number of unemployed people is an important signal of overall economic health because consumer spending is highly correlated with labour-market conditions – released monthly about 30 days after the month ends.

GDP q/q: Change in the inflation-adjusted value of all goods and services produced by the economy. There are 3 versions of GDP released about 20 days apart – Preliminary Flash, Flash, and Revised. The Preliminary Flash release is the earliest and thus tends to have the most impact – released quarterly about 30 days after the quarter ends.

ZEW Economic Sentiment: Level of a diffusion index based on surveyed German institutional investors and analysts. A Survey of about 275 German institutional investors and analysts asks respondents to rate the relative 6-month economic outlook for Germany.

It is a leading indicator of economic health - investors and analysts are highly informed by virtue of their job, and changes in their sentiment can be an early signal of future economic activity – released monthly on the second or third Tuesday of the current month.

Flash Manufacturing PMI: French, German and European level of a diffusion index based on surveyed purchasing managers in the manufacturing industry. It is a leading indicator of economic health as businesses react quickly to market conditions, and their purchasing managers hold perhaps the most current and relevant insight into the company's view of the economy.

There are 2 versions of this report released about a week apart – Flash and Final. The Flash release is the earliest and thus tends to have the most impact – released monthly around 3 weeks into the current month.

CPI y/y: Change in the price of goods and services purchased by consumers. There are 2 versions of this report released about two weeks apart, Flash and Final. The Flash report is extremely early and tends to have a significant impact. Flash is released monthly, on the last business day of the current month.

Retail Sales m/m: Change in the total value of sales at the retail level. It is the primary gauge of consumer spending, which accounts for most of the overall economic activity – released monthly about 35 days after the month ends.

GREAT BRITAIN

Unemployment Rate: Percentage of the total workforce that is unemployed and actively seeking employment during the previous three months. Although it is generally viewed as a lagging indicator, the number of unemployed people is an important signal of overall economic health because consumer spending is highly correlated with labour-market conditions – released monthly about 45 days after the month ends.

Average Earnings: Change in the price businesses and the government pay for labour, including bonuses. It is a leading indicator of consumer inflation when businesses pay more for labour; the higher costs are usually passed on to the consumer – released monthly about 45 days after the month ends.

GDP q/q: Change in the inflation-adjusted value of all goods and services produced by the economy. There are 3 versions of GDP released a month apart: Preliminary, Second Estimate, and Final.

- Preliminary: It is the earliest and thus tends to have the most impact – released quarterly about 26 days after the quarter ends.
- Second Estimate: Released quarterly about 55 days after the quarter ends.
- Final: Released quarterly about 85 days after the quarter ends.

Manufacturing PMI: Level of a diffusion index based on surveyed purchasing managers in the manufacturing industry. Survey of about 600 purchasing managers which asks respondents to rate the relative level of business conditions including employment, production, new orders, prices, supplier deliveries, and inventories – released monthly on the first business day after the month ends.

CPI y/y: Change in the price of goods and services purchased by consumers. The average price of various goods and services are sampled and then compared to the sampling done a year earlier – released monthly about 16 days after the month ends.

Retail Sales: Released monthly, about 16 days after the month ends. It is the primary gauge of consumer spending, which accounts for most of the overall economic activity – released monthly about 20 days after the month ends.

Construction PMI: Level of a diffusion index based on surveyed purchasing managers in the construction industry. Survey of about 170 purchasing managers which asks respondents to rate the relative level of business conditions including employment, production, new orders, prices, supplier deliveries and inventories. Above 50.0 indicates industry expansion, below indicates contraction – released monthly on the second business day after the month ends.

Service PMI: Level of a diffusion index based on surveyed purchasing managers in the services industry. A Survey of purchasing managers asks respondents to rate the relative level of business conditions including employment, production, new orders, prices, supplier deliveries and inventories. It is very important since the British economy rests heavily on services – released monthly on the third business day after the month ends.

SWITZERLAND

KOF Economic Research: This index is designed to predict the direction of the economy over the next 6 months. A combined reading of 219 economic indicators related to banking confidence, production, new orders, consumer confidence, exchange rate, money supply, interest rate spreads, stock market prices and housing – is released monthly around the end of the current month.

CPI m/m: Change in the price of goods and services purchased by consumers – released monthly about 6 days after the month ends.

PPI m/m: Change in the price of goods and raw materials purchased by manufacturers is released monthly about 14 days after the month ends.

JAPAN

GDP q/q: Change in the inflation-adjusted value of all goods and services produced by the economy. There are 2 versions of GDP release:

- Preliminary: It is the earliest and thus tends to have the most impact – released quarterly about 45 days after the quarter ends.
- Final: Released quarterly about 70 days after the quarter ends.

Manufacturing Index: Level of a diffusion index based on surveyed large manufacturers. This survey is used to predict the BOJ's Tankan survey which is released about a week later – released quarterly about 70 days into the current quarter.

BOJ's Tankan: This is a quarterly poll of business confidence reported by the Bank of Japan showing the status of the Japanese economy. It is one of the key financial measures in Japan and has considerable influence on the currency rate – released quarterly around the end of the current quarter.

AUSTRALIA

Unemployment Change: Change in the number of employed people during the previous month. Job creation is an important leading indicator of consumer spending, which accounts for most of the overall economic activity – released monthly about 15 days after the month ends.

Unemployment Rate: Percentage of the total workforce that is unemployed and actively seeking employment during the previous month – released monthly about 15 days after the month ends.

GDP: Change in the inflation-adjusted value of all goods and services produced by the economy – released quarterly about 65 days after the quarter ends.

CPI q/q: Change in the price of goods and services purchased by consumers – released quarterly about 25 days after the quarter ends.

Retail Sales m/m: Change in the total value of sales at the retail level – released monthly about 35 days after the month ends.

Building Approvals: Change in the number of new building approvals issued. It is an excellent gauge of future construction activity because obtaining government approval is among the first steps in constructing a new building. Construction is important because it produces a wide-reaching ripple effect, for example, jobs are created for the construction workers, subcontractors and inspectors are hired, and various services are purchased by the builder – released monthly about 30 days after the month ends.

Trade Balance: Difference in value between imported and exported goods during the reported month. Export demand and currency demand are directly linked because foreigners must buy the domestic currency to pay for the nation's exports. Export demand also impacts production and prices at domestic manufacturers. A positive number indicates that more goods were exported than imported – released monthly about 35 days after the month ends.

NEW ZEALAND

Unemployment Rate: Percentage of the total workforce that is unemployed and actively seeking employment during the previous quarter – released quarterly about 35 days after the quarter ends.

GDP q/q: Change in the inflation-adjusted value of all goods and services produced by the economy – released quarterly about 80 days after the quarter ends.

CPI q/q: Change in the price of goods and services purchased by consumers –

released quarterly about 18 days after the quarter ends.

PPI q/q: Change in the price of goods and raw materials purchased by manufacturers – released quarterly about 50 days after the quarter ends.

Retail Sales: Change in the total value of inflation-adjusted sales at the retail level – released quarterly about 45 days after the quarter ends.

CHINA

GDP q/q: Change in the inflation-adjusted value of all goods and services produced by the economy. It is the broadest measure of economic activity and the primary gauge of the economy's health. Data represents the quarterly value compared to the same quarter a year earlier. Chinese data can have a broad impact on the currency markets due to China's influence on the global economy and investor sentiment – released quarterly about 18 days after the quarter ends.

Unemployment Rate: Percentage of the total urban workforce that is unemployed and actively seeking employment during the previous month. Although it is generally viewed as a lagging indicator, the number of unemployed people is an important signal of overall economic health because consumer spending is highly correlated with labour-market conditions. Unemployment is also a major consideration for those steering the country's monetary policy- released monthly, excluding February about 15 days after the month ends.

Industrial Production: Change in the total inflation-adjusted value of output produced by manufacturers, mines, and utilities. It is a leading indicator of economic health - production is the dominant driver of the economy and reacts quickly to ups and downs in the business cycle – released monthly, excluding Feb about 15 days after the month ends.

Manufacturing PMI: Level of a diffusion index based on surveyed purchasing managers in the manufacturing industry. A survey of 3,000 purchasing managers asks respondents to rate the relative level of business conditions including employment, production, new orders, prices, supplier deliveries, and inventories.

It is a leading indicator of the economic health of businesses that react quickly to market conditions, and their purchasing managers hold perhaps the most current and relevant insight into the company's view of the economy.

It tends to have more impact when it is released ahead of the Caixin Manufacturing PMI because the reports are tightly correlated – released monthly, on the last day of the current month.

Caixin Service PMI: Level of a diffusion index based on surveyed purchasing managers in the services industry. A survey of about 400 purchasing managers asks respondents to rate the relative level of business conditions including employment, production, new orders, prices, supplier deliveries, and inventories.

It is a leading indicator of the economic health of businesses that react quickly to market conditions, and their purchasing managers hold perhaps the most current and relevant insight into the company's view of the economy – released monthly on the third business day after the month ends.

CPI y/y: Change in the price of goods and services purchased by consumers. Consumer prices account for most of the overall inflation. Inflation is important to currency valuation because rising prices lead the central bank to respond by raising interest rates. The average price of various goods and services are sampled and then compared to the sampling done a year earlier – released monthly usually about 10 days after the month ends.

PPI y/y: Change in the price of goods purchased and sold by producers. It is a leading indicator of consumer inflation when producers pay and charge more for goods the higher costs are usually passed on to the consumer – released monthly usually about 10 days after the month ends.

Trade Balance: The difference in value between imported and exported goods during the previous month. Export demand and currency demand are directly linked because foreigners usually buy domestic currency to pay for the nation's exports. Export demand also impacts the production and prices of domestic manufacturers – released monthly about 10 days after the month ends.

TRADE FLOWS AND CAPITAL FLOWS

CHAPTER 9

~

This book explains in detail how to analyse a currency pair, clearly and coherently so that you have all the information you need to trade currencies and make a profit. To do this I will also have to cover, for your better understanding of the whole analytical process, aspects that are relative to currency trading but often ignored, as you saw with macroeconomics in Chapter 7 and will see in this chapter why it is imperative to look at some under the radar factors that influence your currency pairs in the medium to long-term.

I will try to do this in a simple and brief way, to give you enough background to understand why you should consider them as you begin putting your trading process together. If you want to go deeper into certain concepts or economic dynamics, there are specific books that might be of interest to you on this subject.

In the previous chapter we learnt that the biggest currency manipulators are the central banks. However, their decisions will only take effect in the medium to long-term, as it will take time for the change in certain economic forces to have a real effect on the economy.

Primarily, fundamentals are grouped into two broad sub-categories: Trade Flows and Capital Flows.

Trade Flows

The exchange of goods and services between one country and another generates capital movements between the two countries. Trade Flows represent the trade balance, i.e., the number of goods and services a country sells to other countries (exports) minus the number of goods and services it buys (imports).

Countries that export more than they import have a trade surplus. The demand for that country's currency increases because international customers have to buy the country's currency to purchase these goods. This also increases the value of the currency.

Conversely, countries that import more than they export have a trade deficit. In order to buy goods from other countries, importers have to sell their own currency and buy foreign currency. This causes a decrease in the value of the national currency.

An example is Australia. Australia exports more goods to countries – especially China – than it imports from international producers; it has a current account surplus of 2.3% of GDP [December 2021 data]. This creates an international demand to buy AUD so that international customers can buy Australian products.

As you will see in Chapter 20, the Australian dollar is a "Commodity Currency", that is, a currency whose economy is based on the export of commodities. This allows it to have a financial surplus and is the main reason why AUD will not depreciate sharply.

Clearly, a change in the balance of payments from one country to another has a direct effect on currency levels. Therefore, it is important for traders to keep abreast of economic data regarding this balance and understand the implications of changes in the balance of payments.

Important! The trade balance reflects greater or lesser demand for a currency and can influence currency exchange rates.

Capital Flows

Similar in some ways to Trade Flows above, Capital Flows measure the net amount of a currency that is bought or sold for capital investments, especially bonds and shares. The key concept behind capital flows is equilibrium. For example, a country may have positive or negative capital flows.

A positive balance of capital flows implies that investments entering a country from foreign sources exceed investments leaving that country for foreign sources. When capital inflows exceed outflows, this leads to an increase in the demand for currency. This demand increases the value of that currency because a foreign investor must change his currency to that of the country where he is depositing his money.

A negative capital flow balance indicates that investments leaving a country from foreign sources exceed investments entering a country from foreign sources. When there is a negative capital flow, there is less demand for that country's currency, which makes it lose value. This is because the investor has to sell his currency to buy the currency of the country where he is depositing his money.

Countries that offer the highest return on investment through high interest rates, economic growth, and growing financial markets tend to attract the most foreign capital. These countries maintain a positive capital flow. If a country's stock market is doing well and offers a high interest rate, foreign sources are likely to send capital to that country. This increases the demand for that currency and ensures that its value appreciates.

Foreign capital tends to flow into countries that have strong governments, dynamic economies, and stable currencies. A country needs a relatively stable currency to attract capital from foreign investors. Otherwise, the prospect of exchange rate losses caused by currency depreciation may discourage foreign investors.

Let me give you an example with the UK and the US. The US has a strong economy, with the stock market at highs and several interest rates rises planned for 2022. The UK, on the other hand, has a weak economy with a dearth of investment opportunities.

In this scenario, UK investors sell pounds and buy US dollars to take advantage of the better conditions and opportunities in the US market. Hence:

- Capital flows from the UK to the US.
- Demand for GBP decreases and demand for USD increases.
- The value of GBP decreases in relation to the value of USD.

A strategy that is widely used by hedge funds, and which you will see in detail in Chapter 25, is the carry trade.

In conclusion, with this brief overview of trade balance and trade flows/capital flows, it is now clear to you how this type of information works and why a Forex trader would do well to follow these money flows. Because if, as mentioned at the beginning of this chapter, in the medium to long term it is central banks that move currencies, in the short to very short term it is speculation and international trade that dictates law.

ECONOMIC PROJECTIONS

CHAPTER 10

~

In the Economic projections, there are the basic points of the American economy, which are revised every three months. It is very important because it gives you a clearer vision of the forecast and, therefore, of what the market expects. If these expectations are not met, the market will tend to react negatively, and that will weaken the USD.

Let's see the table of the Economic Projections released on December 14, 2016 (Figure 4).

For release at 2:00 p.m., EST, December 14, 2016

Economic projections of Federal Reserve Board members and Federal Reserve Bank presidents under their individual assessments of projected appropriate monetary policy, December 2016
Advance release of table 1 of the Summary of Economic Projections to be released with the FOMC minutes

Percent

Variable	Median[1]					Central tendency[2]					Range[3]				
	2016	2017	2018	2019	Longer run	2016	2017	2018	2019	Longer run	2016	2017	2018	2019	Longer run
Change in real GDP	1.9	2.1	2.0	1.9	1.8	1.8−1.9	1.9−2.3	1.8−2.2	1.8−2.0	1.8−2.0	1.8−2.0	1.7−2.4	1.7−2.3	1.5−2.2	1.6−2.2
September projection	1.8	2.0	2.0	1.8	1.8	1.7−1.9	1.9−2.2	1.8−2.1	1.7−2.0	1.7−2.0	1.7−2.0	1.6−2.5	1.5−2.3	1.6−2.2	1.6−2.2
Unemployment rate	4.7	4.5	4.5	4.5	4.8	4.7−4.8	4.5−4.6	4.3−4.7	4.3−4.8	4.7−5.0	4.7−4.8	4.4−4.7	4.2−4.7	4.1−4.8	4.5−5.0
September projection	4.8	4.6	4.5	4.6	4.8	4.7−4.9	4.5−4.7	4.4−4.7	4.4−4.8	4.7−5.0	4.7−4.9	4.4−4.8	4.3−4.9	4.2−5.0	4.5−5.0
PCE inflation	1.5	1.9	2.0	2.0	2.0	1.5	1.7−2.0	1.9−2.0	2.0−2.1	2.0	1.5−1.6	1.7−2.0	1.8−2.2	1.8−2.2	2.0
September projection	1.3	1.9	2.0	2.0	2.0	1.2−1.4	1.7−1.9	1.8−2.0	1.9−2.0	2.0	1.1−1.7	1.5−2.0	1.8−2.0	1.8−2.1	2.0
Core PCE inflation[4]	1.7	1.8	2.0	2.0		1.7−1.8	1.8−1.9	1.9−2.0	2.0		1.6−1.8	1.7−2.0	1.8−2.2	1.8−2.2	
September projection	1.7	1.8	2.0	2.0		1.6−1.8	1.7−1.9	1.9−2.0	2.0		1.5−2.0	1.6−2.0	1.8−2.0	1.8−2.1	
Memo: Projected appropriate policy path															
Federal funds rate	0.6	1.4	2.1	2.9	3.0	0.6	1.1−1.6	1.9−2.6	2.4−3.3	2.8−3.0	0.6	0.9−2.1	0.9−3.4	0.9−3.9	2.5−3.8
September projection	0.6	1.1	1.9	2.6	2.9	0.6−0.9	1.1−1.8	1.9−2.8	2.4−3.0	2.8−3.0	0.4−1.1	0.6−2.1	0.6−3.1	0.6−3.8	2.5−3.8

NOTE: Projections of change in real gross domestic product (GDP) and projections for both measures of inflation are percent changes from the fourth quarter of the previous year to the fourth quarter of the year indicated. PCE inflation and core PCE inflation are the percentage rates of change in, respectively, the price index for personal consumption expenditures (PCE) and the price index for PCE excluding food and energy. Projections for the unemployment rate are for the average civilian unemployment rate in the fourth quarter of the year indicated. Each participant's projections are based on his or her assessment of appropriate monetary policy. Longer-run projections represent each participant's assessment of the rate to which each variable would be expected to converge under appropriate monetary policy and in the absence of further shocks to the economy. The projections for the federal funds rate are the value of the midpoint of the projected appropriate target range for the federal funds rate or the projected appropriate target level for the federal funds rate at the end of the specified calendar year or over the longer run. The September projections were made in conjunction with the meeting of the Federal Open Market Committee on September 20-21, 2016. One participant did not submit longer-run projections for the change in real GDP, the unemployment rate, or the federal funds rate in conjunction with the September 20-21, 2016, meeting, and one participant did not submit such projections in conjunction with the December 13-14, 2016, meeting.
 1. For each period, the median is the middle projection when the projections are arranged from lowest to highest. When the number of projections is even, the median is the average of the two middle projections.
 2. The central tendency excludes the three highest and three lowest projections for each variable in each year.
 3. The range for a variable in a given year includes all participants' projections, from lowest to highest, for that variable in that year.
 4. Longer-run projections for core PCE inflation are not collected.

Figure 4 - Economic Projections December 2016

What can you deduce from it? Here you see described the <u>GDP</u> expected in 2016, 2017, 2018 and 2019, as it was the past projection (September). As you can see, the GDP was revised slightly upwards except for 2018 (unchanged). This means, that the Fed expects an acceleration of the US economy in the future.

That was also one of the catalysts that pushed EURUSD downward in January before other dynamics replaced it. Why? Because a future target had been revised upwards, thus the market was satisfied; therefore, the US Dollar was bought and consequently, the EUR/USD fell.

The next entry is the <u>Unemployment Rate</u> and here, except for 2018 which remained unchanged, for all other years the rate was revised downwards from the September projection.

Another point, with regards to data on employment, the wages (Average Hourly Earnings) hold much importance. If wages do not increase, there is no healthy growth in employment, and therefore, inflation will not rise. The number of employees can grow, but if they do not increase their purchasing power (their wages), you make little progress. That is one of the key points, and I always advise you to keep it in strong consideration in your analysis.

Moving on, you have <u>PCE inflation</u> which has seen, for the year 2016, a rise in the September forecast from 1.3 to 1.5 and this was the second important reason that has led to a strengthening of the US Dollar.

The increase in inflation relative to 2016 is a consequence of the appreciation of different commodities, especially crude oil.

The next entry is the <u>Core PCE Inflation</u>, and this is inflation without the energy component, in fact, the speech confirmed that it remained unchanged both for 2016 and for all subsequent years. That is because, by excluding the energy, the other factors are easier to control.

The last point that you must consider which helped the markets in their bullish trends is the prospect of increased interest rates. You can see this entry under <u>Federal Funds Rate</u> – if the rate was previously planned for 2017 to 1.1 now is expected to be 1.4. That means that in 2017, there will be three rate hikes in the United States. The forecast revised upwards, consequently, also for the next two years.

This programmatic table is reviewed every three months (March, June, September, and December), and on these occasions, there is always a little more attention and more volatility. So, these meetings are much more important than intermediate. The interest rates are much more likely to be raised or cut in one of these four months than those intermediates.

It is essential to understand the expectations of the American economy because the more you know, the more you can understand where the global market can move. Since it will surely have a significant impact on the Dollar, but also on all financial markets - as they are all interconnected - it is therefore very important to know all its aspects in as detailed a manner as possible.

And finally, the table shows, on the top row, three items: Median, Central Tendency, and Range. Below the table, there is an explanation of their meaning. However, do not complicate your analysis too much. You only need to look at the Median because that is where you should focus. If you want to do a study, below the table are all the explanations, again, it is unnecessary as you have plenty of information as it is – you only need to concentrate on the Median data.

In the next chapter, you are going to see some of the most important macroeconomic data, the kind of data that moves markets as well as currencies.

NON-FARM PAYROLLS

CHAPTER 11

~

As introduced, the Non-Farm Payrolls is the data that moves both markets and currencies. Usually released on the first Friday of the month together with two other major data regarding employment: the Unemployment Rate and Average Hourly Earnings.

It is important to read the various industries that make up the report and evaluate them as one component. The data could be lower than expected, but if there has been an increase in employment in any industry the data is equally positive.

You can see an example of Non-Farm Payrolls in Figure 5. The table always has the same structure; therefore, it will always be identical every time. often you can find it on page 5 or 6 of the report, called "Employment by Selected Industry" where you find the employment for each industry and, in the last entry, the Government.

The last two columns are the ones that you pay attention to, in this case, January 2017 and February 2017. You simply glance over the industries - it will help you not only to work with the data but also to have an overview of the industries that are strong or those that show weakness - this visual work can be useful, as it enables you to select securities of a specific industry easily.

The first thing you need to do is to start the analysis with "Mining and logging"; this is the hardest industry of all.

The data, as you can see, is showing obvious signs of improvement and the industry is producing new employment. This data also tells us: that if you are thinking of investing in securities (or options) in mining, they may have a decent price increase, by virtue of an improvement in employment and thus the expansion of the industry.

Bear in mind that a big part of the increase in employment is due to oil prices, in relation to the extractions that were made. The crude oil price from November to early March 2016 grew by more than 20%, consequently, the workers have also increased.

Summary table B. Establishment data, seasonally adjusted

Category	Feb. 2016	Dec. 2016	Jan. 2017p	Feb. 2017p
EMPLOYMENT BY SELECTED INDUSTRY (Over-the-month change, in thousands)				
Total nonfarm	237	155	238	235
Total private	221	150	221	227
Goods-producing	-7	32	54	95
Mining and logging	-18	2	3	9
Construction	23	12	40	58
Manufacturing	-12	18	11	28
Durable goods[1]	-13	13	7	10
Motor vehicles and parts	1.2	0.9	2.7	-3.5
Nondurable goods	1	5	4	18
Private service-providing	228	118	167	132
Wholesale trade	-1.5	1.6	5.9	9.9
Retail trade	48.4	13.3	39.9	-26.0
Transportation and warehousing	3.2	13.4	-10.2	8.8
Utilities	0.7	0.2	-0.4	-1.0
Information	10	-6	-3	0
Financial activities	6	22	32	7
Professional and business services[1]	25	36	46	37
Temporary help services	-6.7	-17.4	6.5	3.1
Education and health services[1]	74	50	21	62
Health care and social assistance	52.0	39.2	26.1	32.5
Leisure and hospitality	45	5	24	26
Other services	17	-17	12	8
Government	16	5	17	8
(3-month average change, in thousands)				
Total nonfarm	201	148	186	209
Total private	183	153	183	199
WOMEN AND PRODUCTION AND NONSUPERVISORY EMPLOYEES AS A PERCENT OF ALL EMPLOYEES[2]				
Total nonfarm women employees	49.5	49.6	49.6	49.6
Total private women employees	48.0	48.2	48.1	48.2
Total private production and nonsupervisory employees	82.4	82.4	82.5	82.5
HOURS AND EARNINGS ALL EMPLOYEES Total private				
Average weekly hours	34.5	34.4	34.4	34.4
Average hourly earnings	$25.38	$25.98	$26.03	$26.09
Average weekly earnings	$875.61	$893.71	$895.43	$897.50
Index of aggregate weekly hours (2007=100)[3]	105.1	106.2	106.4	106.6
Over-the-month percent change	-0.1	0.4	0.2	0.2
Index of aggregate weekly payrolls (2007=100)[4]	127.5	131.9	132.4	133.0
Over-the-month percent change	0.0	0.7	0.4	0.5
DIFFUSION INDEX (Over 1-month span)[5]				
Total private (261 industries)	58.6	60.0	58.0	63.0
Manufacturing (78 industries)	48.1	53.8	50.0	65.4

[1] Includes other industries, not shown separately.

[2] Data relate to production employees in mining and logging and manufacturing, construction employees in construction, and nonsupervisory employees in the service-providing industries.

[3] The indexes of aggregate weekly hours are calculated by dividing the current month's estimates of aggregate hours by the corresponding annual average aggregate hours.

[4] The indexes of aggregate weekly payrolls are calculated by dividing the current month's estimates of aggregate weekly payrolls by the corresponding annual average aggregate weekly payrolls.

[5] Figures are the percent of industries with employment increasing plus one-half of the industries with unchanged employment, where 50 percent indicates an equal balance between industries with increasing and decreasing employment.

p Preliminary

NOTE: Data have been revised to reflect March 2016 benchmark levels and updated seasonal adjustment factors.

Figure 5 - Non-Farm Payrolls February 2017

Below "Mining and logging" you find all other industries, and although the data was less than the previous month, there was no loss of employment or crises, but only a moment of transition. Even the "Retail trade" that has seen a decline in employment of 23K, is coming from a significant increase in January of nearly 40K. With experience, you will realise that retail trade is the only industry that is important to track regularly.

The data shows consistency, it is in line with the previous month and does not show any alarm bell – no industry is growing too fast, and no crisis is present, if there were any discrepancies it would be considered as a red flag.

Just looking at the table (Figure 5) gives you a complete overview of the data – like any piece of information, you need to extract key figures to draw your conclusion as I have shown you earlier - you can visit the "U.S. <u>Bureau of Labour Statistics</u>" website. As you open the file, read the release on the data, especially the first three-four lines given as a summary on the first page in the employment situation headline. However, my advice is to read further "<u>Establishment Survey Data</u>" which I reproduce below:

"*Total Non-Farm Payrolls employment increased by 235,000 in February. Job gains occurred in construction, private educational services, manufacturing, health care and mining.*"

I prefer to see the Non-Farm Payrolls split up into the different industries because, in this way, I have a broader and more complete view.

Undoubtedly, NFP data releases are associated with sharp moves in the market that could swing either side – after the initial move (the end of euphoria) and once the data has been digested by market participants – you can enter a trade like professional traders at the investment banks as you have the correct reading and a bit of time to reflect on what the numbers mean.

<u>In conclusion</u>, when the data of the Non-Farm Payrolls come out, the first movement is emotional, depending on the data value. You must do an accurate reading of the data, industries, and quality of wages (Average Hourly Earnings) and this is the reason why, often, you can expect a reversal of EURUSD (as well as other currency pairs).

CORRELATION IN FOREX

CHAPTER 12

∼

Let us see another concept: correlation. Correlation is defined as the ratio of price developments of two markets. Simply put correlated markets are when one market increases in price it has a knock-on effect on the second market thus price increase and vice versa – and quite often a decline of the first market will correspond with a decline in the second one.

The correlation coefficient is a measure that determines the magnitude of strength or weakness between two markets. The range of values for the correlation coefficient is -1.0 to 1.0. If a calculated correlation is greater than 1.0 or less than -1.0, the calculation is flawed. A correlation of 1.0 indicates a perfect positive correlation, while a correlation of -1.0 indicates a perfect negative correlation. 0.0 means that the two markets have no correlation; they are independent of each other.

When we speak of correlation between currencies, we refer to the movement of two currency pairs, which can go in tandem, against, or randomly according to a certain period of time. As currencies trade in pairs, it is not possible for one currency to move without affecting the other.

Are the correlations important? It depends, in Forex no. Indeed, correlations are very often harmful, and I will explain the reasons why.

First of all, correlations come and go. It means that today two currency pairs can be correlated, but tomorrow they may not be. Looking at the correlations in different timeframes, we could see different values, precisely because they are not stable.

Therefore, setting a strategy based on the degree of correlation between the different currency pairs, it is likely that suddenly that correlation ceases – and the worst thing is, you only realise it when you incur losses, without having the opportunity to modify the trade first.

"If EURUSD rises, then GBPUSD will rise as well." Probable but it is not certain because when you create a currency pair, you do nothing but oppose two economies, and the Eurozone economy is vastly different from the UK economy. Not only it is hard to evaluate two economies well, but also by adding a correlation factor to a third economy – your analysis becomes very complicated.

A statement like "if you know the correlations, you can cover yourself in case of a loss" is blatantly wrong. The foolish thing to do if you are long on EURUSD is to cover yourselves by selling USDCHF. You might as well close the position because, in the positive outcome, the loss is kept steady, in the negative outcome, it increases the losses because the correlation does not work.

The best thing to do if you want to protect your portfolio is to use safe-haven currencies, which you will discover in the following chapters.

The same goes for the diversification of the portfolio. "Instead of investing $ 20,000 on a long trade on AUDUSD, you can invest $ 10,000 on the long of AUDUSD and $ 10,000 on the long of NZDUSD." However, the above is not always a good strategy. The Australian and New Zealand economies are similar but different in some respects, such as, for example, the monetary policy. There are better ways to diversify a Forex portfolio.

The essential correlations that every Forex trader must know are those between currencies and commodities. Some economies are mainly based on the export of commodities. The currencies of these countries are called Commodity Currencies. The currencies most traded that belong to this category are CAD (Canadian Dollar), AUD (Australian Dollar), and NZD (New Zealand Dollar).

I finish the chapter by saying that I do not use correlations between currencies in my trading, but everyone is free to think differently. For those interested in the Myfxbook website (https://www.myfxbook.com/forex-market/correlation), you can find the correlation table. You can select the time frame and currency pairs of your interest.

You can verify the correlation values once you input the percentile you wish as it changes according to the time you choose from 1 day, 1 week, to 1 month. The same is the case for smaller time frames.

THE OPERATIONAL PLAN

CHAPTER 13

~

The scenario that you have created becomes a starting point not only for the analysis of currencies but also as a fundamental step for balancing and consolidating your portfolio positions. Your goal is to buy currencies with the greatest strengths and to sell the ones that are subject to adverse scenarios.

This is a basic concept, and I have already repeated it. It is the cornerstone of the entire analysis, which otherwise would not make sense. All your work is focused on analysing the two economies (the two currencies that make up the currency pair) to establish with certainty which of the two is the strongest, and therefore, what will be the future movement of the currency pair (as long as the initial assumption does not change).

So, how do you execute the scenario that you have built? First, you acknowledge the key points and levels you have defined at the start of your analysis. Then, you draw the sensitive level on the chart where news, reports and speeches have created these price movements or will move the price in a particular way.

I am talking about support and resistance levels, both technical and fundamental, which you will see better in the following two chapters. As said, supports and resistances are the only aspect of technical analysis I use in my analysis.

I like to set up wide-ranging operations, as I like to make sure that I can manage the operation so that even though there is a movement against my position, this does not put me in trouble. I open my first order for testing the market, a "spy order" you could also call it probing the market, usually a small amount, of course, always proportionate to the whole position. Personally, for the spy order, I use 1/4 of the entire position (however, never more than 1/3).

Then, I open a higher primary order concerning the size, just to rebalance the average price and be able to better ride the operation (obviously, the whole order must respect my position sizing).

Why more than one market entry? Because one market entry with the whole position, you risk putting a stop-loss much closer, which would mean that managing the position would become much more inconvenient than just splitting the market entry with a first spy order, followed by a primary order.

The size of the spy order, however, should not be too small but rather fruitful in case the price does not reach the level of the primary order. You must be proportionate in what you do. The spy order cannot be too small or large because the parameters of the operation are wide-ranging.

In addition to the market entry, you also need to establish stop-loss and target profit levels. The stop loss is mainly mathematical because the first thing you look for is your capital. You cannot invest a percentage that overwhelms your risk management. Hence your stop loss should be based on what you want to risk according to your capital size.

While the stop-loss level is fixed and *irremovable* (to the level you chose to close the trade) according to your profit target, I usually like to see how the currency pair comes to that profit target, and if there is room for making the trade run a little more (or whether it is wiser to close it early). That is the reason why I do not want to give any rules, because the markets are not the same every day, and the plan can change at any time.

Conversely, a stop-loss must never be modified, or rather, if you move it to reduce risk, it is always positive, but once you decided on an exit level, you must respect it. This is also because, by working with a stop loss on the capital, moving the stop-loss means increasing the loss that you had decided in your trading plan, and this does not make you feel more comfortable with that trade.

How do you decide when to open the primary order? Once the spy order is executed, you could see the development of the price action and the possible scenarios you anticipated. Let me give an example: you sell EURUSD. If the currency pair falls, it goes to your advantage, meaning the spy order will gain you a profit. If the market rises, then you will choose an excess level where to open the primary order. An excess level, that is above the "fundamental resistance" created by a decision of the central bank.

Here, you are faced with another concept inherent in investment banks, the subjective probability which is the numeric measure of chance (probability) that reflects the degree of a personal belief in the likelihood of an occurrence.

In my two years as a fund manager, I changed my mentality and understood the importance of subjective probability for market entry - contrary to what you read on the internet. Chapter 19 is dedicated to subjective probability to expand on this argument.

In conclusion, your aim is the sensitive level, but you must consider the excess level when it's applicable and never be satisfied with the current price because you can reap additional benefits from it in the market. The next chapter will clarify a lot of these levels for you, so you fully understand the concept that I use in my own trading.

TECHNICAL SUPPORT & RESISTANCE

CHAPTER 14

~

Note, that I do not use technical analysis. The subjective probability (which will be discussed later) gives me the entry points. However, this chapter helps me explain the differences between technical and fundamental supports and resistances.

The key is analysing the existing monetary policy difference between the two economies that suggests which currency pairs offer the most excellent opportunities for trading, at any given time. Your goal is to evaluate daily market conditions and, eventually, modify the strategy accordingly if and when something changes.

The first step is to study macroeconomics on a global scale. You need to establish the backdrop at the highest level and filter the data to arrive at the dynamics of currency pairs at the lowest level. In doing so, you will examine the monetary policies of major central banks and a few other indicators (the most relevant). It is very important that you only weigh the data, without giving importance to the rumours.

It is vital to understand the different monetary policies of central banks and analyse the economic developments of a country through its macroeconomic data.

Nevertheless, once you have done a comprehensive analysis of two economies, that gives you a good insight into which economy (and therefore currency) is stronger - it does not give you the ideal market entry (timing).

If for example, you have established that the Canadian economy is expanding, while New Zealand is in a contraction phase, it does not mean that NZDCAD will fall tomorrow. What you must do is look for a good entry level to open a bearish position on the currency pair.

What I do, is search on the chart for a resistance level where NZDCAD is not "insensitive", a special zone that represents an excellent market entry (even though there are other considerations to make).

Before moving on to some practical examples, let us look at various types of supports and resistances. Here are the definitions again.

A level is defined as "support" when the demand is particularly strong, and sellers cannot overwhelm it. A support level is even more significant if in the past it has been tested multiple times without breaking. So, the support reflects the inability of a market to drop below a certain price level. Below, you can see an example of support with the EURGBP daily chart (Figure 6).

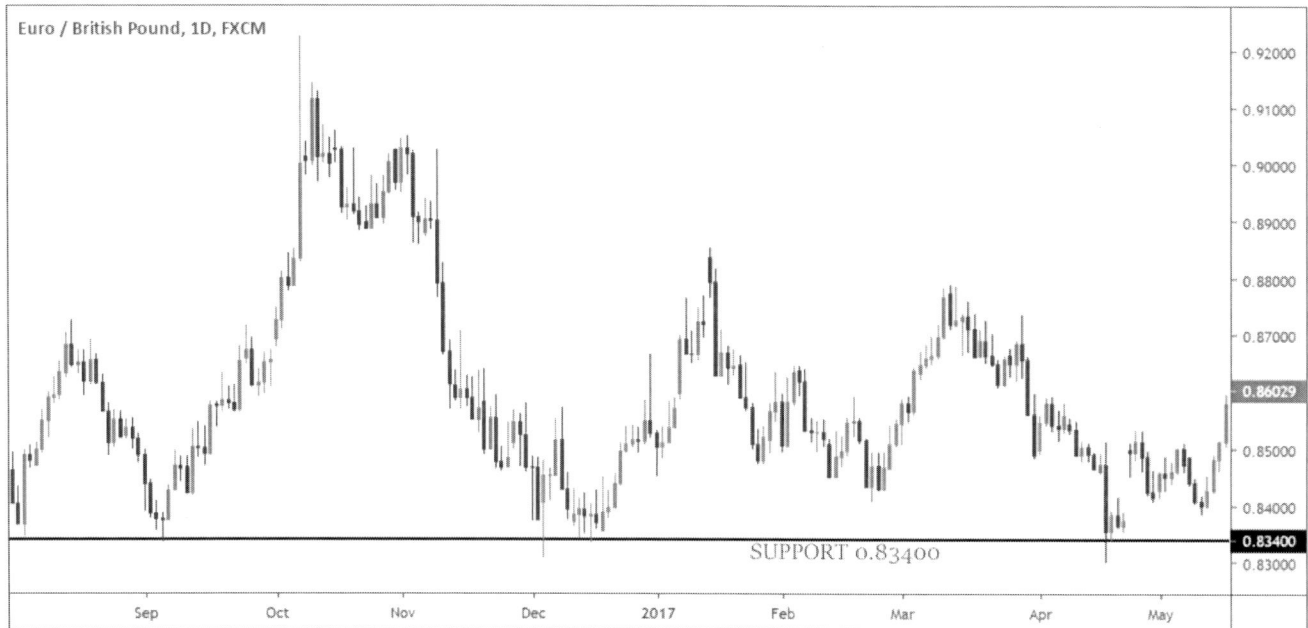

Figure 6 - EURGBP daily chart with support (TradingView.com)

A level is defined as "resistance" when the offer is particularly strong, and buyers cannot win against sellers. A resistance level becomes more significant the more times it has been tested without breaking.

So, the resistance reflects the inability of a market to climb above a certain price level – an example of resistance with the AUDCAD daily chart (Figure 7).

There are two types of support/resistance: static and dynamic.

- A "static" support/resistance level corresponds to a precise and constant point in time, such as the high and low of the year, or a Fibonacci retracement (you will come across these in a minute).

- A "dynamic" support/resistance level, however, its value changes as time passes.

Figure 7 - AUDCAD daily chart with resistance (TradingView.com)

Supports and resistances over time tend to be overcome, in such cases, an old resistance becomes new support, and past support turns into new resistance. There is a *change of polarity*, as shown above in the NZDJPY weekly chart (Figure 8).

Figure 8 - NZDJPY weekly chart change of polarity (TradingView.com)

Fibonacci retracements provide the second type of static support and resistance. Fibonacci retracements consist of horizontal intervals that correspond to Fibonacci levels such as 23.6%, 38.2%, 50%, and 61.8%.

The Fibonacci retracements can be considered supports and resistances, as shown in the USDCAD daily chart (Figure 9). Observe how the price meets resistance on 50% Fibonacci retracement. If you look at the downtrend of USDCAD, you can easily see that every time the currency pair rebounds, the retracement ends at a Fibonacci level (23.8% or 38%).

Figure 9 - USDCAD daily chart with Fibonacci (TradingView.com)

It will not always be so, especially because you do not know where a currency pair will stop the rebound (38.2% 50% or maybe 61.8). But that is common for all the static resistances (and supports).

Another type of static support and resistance is given by the highs and lows of the previous years. Often, they are significant levels where the market is not insensitive as shown in Figure 10 with the chart of AUDUSD – drawing the lows and highs of previous years on the chart can be an excellent way, particularly for beginners, to find important levels that the market will find hard to overcome.

FX:AUDUSD, 1D 0.69776 ▼ −0.00432 (−0.62%) O:0.70208 H:0.70288 L:0.69575 C:0.69776

Figure 10 - AUDUSD daily chart (TradingView.com)

Gaps aka windows in the candlestick analysis, are another static level that often sees the formation of supports and resistances. The gaps in forex are sporadic and can occur only between the close of Friday and the open of Sunday.

FX:GBPCAD, 1D 1.63781 ▼ −0.00340 (−0.21%) O:1.64121 H:1.64446 L:1.63669 C:1.63781

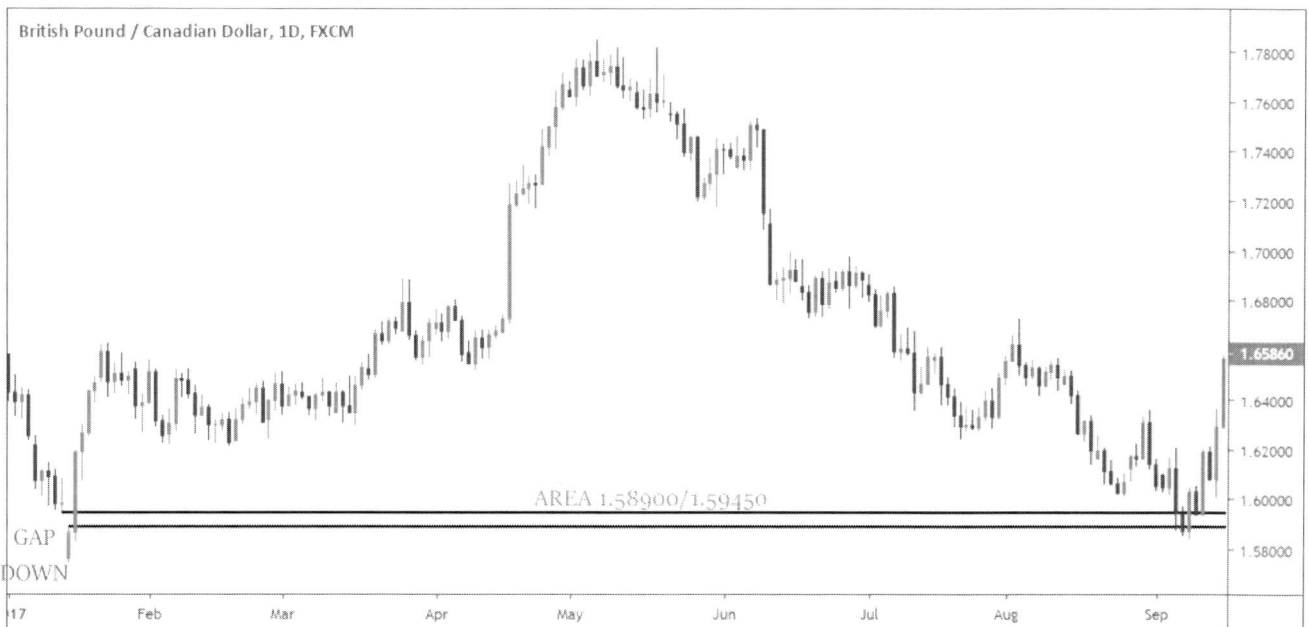

Figure 11 - GBPCAD daily chart (TradingView.com)

Very often, the gaps hide the willingness of the currency pair to go in the opposite direction as the chart above of GBPCAD in Figure 11 shows where, after the gap down, the currency pair has risen by about 900 pips in a few days.

Now, let's see the dynamic support and resistance. The most used is the trendline. A line that follows the lows (support) or the highs (resistance) of a trend, as you can see in Figure 12 with the EURCHF daily chart.

Figure 12 - EURCHF daily chart (TradingView.com)

The second commonly used way of finding dynamic supports and resistances is the moving average.

A moving average is an indicator used by traders that is based on historical price trends. A moving average is calculated on a certain quantity of price data (period) and is "moving" because it moves from day to day (or other timeframe) precisely because of its calculation method.

So, by way of example, if you want to calculate a 20-day moving average of the EURUSD price, to update it, it will be enough to add to the series the data of today's close, eliminating the close price of 20 days ago.

In practical terms, a 20-day moving average represents the average value of the last 20 trading sessions, and each data will weigh 1/20 of the series. The longer the period you are considering, the less the data that you gradually add will affect the moving average. Thus, a 20-day moving average will be less affected by new data than a 5 day moving average, and more than a 100 day moving average.

Figure 13 below shows the AUDNZD chart to which has been applied the 200-day simple moving average.

Figure 13 - AUDNZD daily chart with 200-day moving average (TradingView.com)

Generally, the 200-day moving average is used as a watershed between bullish and bearish trends. If a currency pair is above the moving average, it is in an uptrend, if it is below, it is a bearish trend.

Nowadays, all the trading platforms facilitate easy application of graphic data which represents the moving average of a price. And, to visualise them on a chart, you no longer have to worry about using graph paper, pencil and calculator, as the chart analysis pioneers did.

Complementing this introduction on the moving average, I add that there are different kinds of them depending on the formula used.

The Simple Moving Average (SMA) is the classic one, the one you have seen above. The Exponential Moving Average (EMA) and the Weighted Moving Average (WMA) are the others most utilised.

As said, in the Simple Moving Average (SMA), each data will get the same weight in the series. If, for example, you use a 14-day SMA, each data will weight 1/14 of the series.

The Exponential Moving Average (EMA) gives more weight to the most recent data. This kind of moving average reacts faster to recent price changes than a simple moving average.

Finally, the Weighted Moving Average (WMA). It gives more weight on recent data and less on past ones (similarly to the Exponential Moving Average). This is done by multiplying every single price by a weighting factor. Because of its unique calculation, WMA will follow prices more closely than a corresponding Simple Moving Average.

Other often-used periods are 21, 34 and 55. You can see an example in Figure 14 with the AUDUSD daily chart with applied the 55-day Exponential Moving Average.

Figure 14 - AUDUSD daily chart with 55-day EMA (TradingView.com)

However, the moving averages work well as dynamic supports and resistances only when the currency pair is in trend – but when the price moves sideways, they become "ineffective"

You can see an example of that in the EURJPY daily chart with the 21-day Simple Moving Average (Figure 15).

FX:EURJPY, 1D 121.740 ▲ +0.092 (+0.08%) O:121.648 H:121.931 L:121.594 C:121.740

Figure 15 - EURJPY daily chart with 21-day SMA (TradingView.com)

In conclusion, static supports and resistances are not part of my subjective probability; however, they can help less-experienced traders find some sensitive levels of a currency pair.

To reiterate, I do not apply technical analysis. I do not consider any pattern or indicator when I work with currencies, I only use support and resistance levels. And if you desire to become a professional trader, you should do the same.

In the next chapter, you are going to see the fundamental supports and resistances, that is, the ones created by the decisions of the Central Banks.

FUNDAMENTAL SUPPORT & RESISTANCE

CHAPTER 15

∾

I mentioned in Chapter 4 (Inside a Currency Pair) that it is vital to analyse a currency pair as two separate economies and I have explained the principle behind it – these two economies carry different factors that need to be considered carefully for proper assessment of currency pair.

Figure 16 - AUDUSD daily chart (TradingView.com)

Now let's see a concrete example with AUDUSD. First, I start analysing the Australian economy, and after I will do the same with the US. My goal is to buy where there is strength and to sell where there is a weakness. Above in Figure 16, you can see the AUDUSD daily chart with two "fundamental" resistances.

On the chart, I highlighted two levels, the first at 0.77000 represents the last cut in Australian interest rates on July 6, 2016. The lower level at 0.7500 is the last hike in interest rates in the US on December 14, 2017 (the latter had already been priced into the market during the previous weeks).

You can also see a static resistance area at 0.77000/0.77500 that has worked perfectly in the past, and from there, AUDUSD has always dropped at a lower price.

Second, I analyse the two individual economies, starting with the <u>Australian</u> one.

PROS:

- Growth in GDP, is expected to be 3% this year.

CONS:

- Exports-based economy. It depends on other economies (China) and the prices of commodities.
- End of the mining investment boom.
- Moderate consumption.
- The continuing slowdown of growth in labour costs means that inflation is expected to remain low for some time.
- An appreciating exchange rate would complicate the growth.

As for the <u>US economy</u> analysis

PROS:

- Domestic consumption-based economy.
- Currency used for international trade.
- Good data regarding employment.
- Economy growing at a faster rate.
- Three projected interest rate hikes in 2017.

CONS:

- Political uncertainty caused by Donald Trump.
- Problems with the budget deficit.
- USD too strong with penalisation on exports.

From the key bullet points above, clearly, the US economy is stronger than the Australian, other things being equal, the US currency will appreciate in the medium-term more than the Australian one. So, the area of 0.77000 is a reasonable level when selling AUDUSD – especially as we have an excess of price.

Notice when we have candles with very long shadows and very tight bodies, it means that the currency pair is in a decision-making phase. The explosion may be very strong, given its nature. The relationship between the commodities (particularly gold and silver) and AUD is very special (you will see this Chapter20).

Correlations such as AUDUSD and gold remain standing on equal terms, but when the variables are changed, specifically interest rates – remember commodities are priced in the US dollar, correlations then no longer exist, nor any other variable should be regarded because the Central Bank decision changes the cards on the table.

Safe to say, correlation works until things remain the same. When the parameters change, the interest rates, in this case, have the advantage of everything else.

Looking at the interest rates, as well as what the central bank does and says is key since it is the central banks that mostly drive the currency pairs. If they leave interest rates unchanged, you can be assured that all the relationships that you have from exports, commodities, and whatever variable it is it will play the conventional way. But if interest rates change, the game changes.

A rate hike is a sign of the strength of the currency (and economy). A rising interest rate puts a stop on inflation. Inflation is generated when the economy proceeds at a fast pace, which means that companies have produced, and continue to produce a lot, this is a healthy labour market. And all of this translates into a great strength for that currency.

In reality, you cannot trade forex if you don't consider the interest rates of currency pairs - they are the basis of what establishes the cost of money. However, when the rates remain unchanged, especially for a long time, the market finds other correlations. In the case of AUDUSD, these correlations are to do with gold, oil and China, due to exportations from Australia.

In the context of the macroeconomic levels (fundamental supports and resistances), sometimes the more volatile the currency pair is the more likely it will overshoot these levels, but they tend to respect them later, in the medium to long-term.

However, sometimes we see a significant spike and that's because they have less liquidity than the "Majors" hence they are more susceptible to higher variations. Always remember, in the short-term, speculation is what moves the markets on all levels.

FX:NZDUSD, 1D 0.66230 ▼ −0.00636 (−0.95%) O:0.66866 H:0.66944 L:0.66021 C:0.66230

New Zealand Dollar / U.S. Dollar, 1D, FXCM

NEW ZEALAND CUTS RATES NOVEMBER 9, 2016   0.73350

USA RISES RATES
DECEMBER 14, 2016   0.72150

0.70416

Oct   Nov   Dec   2017   Feb   Mar

Figure 17 - NZDUSD daily chart (TradingView.com)

FX:USDCAD, 1D 1.30754 ▼ −0.00028 (−0.02%) O:1.30679 H:1.30836 L:1.30613 C:1.30754

U.S. Dollar / Canadian Dollar, 1D, FXCM

1.33530

USA RISES RATES
DECEMBER 14, 2016

CANADA CUTS RATES JULY 15, 2015   1.27280

Apr   May   Jun   Jul   Aug   Sep   Oct   Nov   Dec   2017   Feb   2

Figure 18 – USDCAD daily chart (TradingView.com)

Now, to complete this chapter, let's see a couple of other examples. In Figure 17 above, you can see the NZDUSD daily chart, much the same as what you saw with AUDUSD, but New Zealand is a weaker economy than the Australian one which has led the currency pair to a deeper downward movement.

You find two levels highlighted in the chart. The most recent rate cut in New Zealand, and that of the last rate hike in the United States.

The second example concerns USDCAD You can see the daily chart in Figure 18 above.

Here again, the two fundamental supports highlighted the last rate cut in Canada and the most recent rate hike in the United States have worked very well. That will not be forever as, sooner or later, the conditions will change, but until then, these macroeconomic levels will tend to be respected. And especially what I call "excesses of price" may provide you with excellent opportunities to trade.

SOME MONTHS LATER

CHAPTER 16

∽

You saw how fundamental support and resistance levels form when central banks make monetary policy decisions. These levels are very important and tend to be respected – and from time to time you witness an excess in price (spike) that represents good levels that enable you to open positions.

Figure 19 – EURUSD weekly chart (TradingView.com)

This of course if conditions remain unchanged, when they do change – these levels of fundamental support or resistance may also mean having no more value, which I will demonstrate with an example. Above you find the EURUSD daily chart already seen previously (Figure 19).

And the same chart a few months later (Figure 20).

FX:EURUSD, 1W 1.12302 ▲ +0.00060 (+0.05%) O:1.12261 H:1.12341 L:1.12196 C:1.12302

Figure 20 - EURUSD weekly chart (TradingView.com)

The fundamental resistance levels that had been created by the introduction of Quantitative Easing by the ECB was wiped out. How is this possible? This actually not that surprising. What has happened is that the initial conditions have been modified. On July 20th, at the ECB's meeting, chairman Mario Draghi, responding to a question, implied that the QE might have come to an end: "*in autumn, we should talk about changes to the ECB's stimulus policies.*"

In the September 7 meeting, Draghi confirmed that the QE, in its current form, is going to end in December 2017. Draghi also added that "*the increase in exchange rates is largely endogenous, caused by the strength of the European economy.*" Between the lines, you can read that the Eurozone economy is starting to grow, and that the QE is no longer necessary.

Between the two meetings, on the 25th of August, there were words, or better, what was not said, by the Fed chair Janet Yellen, who did not tackle a discussion on rates of interest, leaving you to infer that the third cut in 2017 is not that certain. So, as you can see, at the monetary policy level, there have been several changes, and these, coupled with the economic performance of the Euro area and of the United States (which you will see more clearly in the next chapter), contributed to the steep rise of EURUSD.

Even the charts seen in the previous chapter have had, at least initially, the same movement, although the motivations were different. If we look at the NZDUSD chart (Figure

21).

FX:NZDUSD, 1D 0.66464 ▲ +0.00234 (+0.35%) O:0.66259 H:0.66531 L:0.66203 C:0.66464

Figure 21 - NZDUSD daily chart (TradingView.com)

The currency pair, from mid-May, began a strong bullish phase that led it to earn about 11%, reaching the resistance at 0.75200.

FX:AUDUSD, 1D 0.69859 ▲ +0.00083 (+0.12%) O:0.69749 H:0.69942 L:0.69743 C:0.69859

Figure 22 - AUDUSD daily chart (TradingView.com)

Then, it dropped from the area of the excess of the price, returning below the level of 0.73400, the fundamental resistance that has been created by the most recent cut in interest rates of the Reserve Bank of New Zealand.

Very similar to the movement of AUDUSD made that you can see in Figure 22. The movement was the same, even though the drop of AUDUSD was slightly less deep, since the Australian economy is stronger than the New Zealand one.

Finally, in Figure 23 you can see a USDCAD daily chart that, due to two interest rate rises decided by the Bank of Canada, has instead continued to fall.

Figure 23 - USDCAD daily chart (TradingView.com)

Only in recent weeks has the currency pair bounced, returning to test the fundamental resistance levels that have formed with the first rise in interest rates decided by the Canadian central bank.

In this chapter, we saw how well key levels of fundamental supports and resistances work until the conditions that led to their formation change. Moreover, some monetary decisions by central banks have led to the removal of a key levels that had been formed over the last two years, to help with the weakening or improvement of the economies of the individual countries.

You have also seen the strong bullish move for NZD, AUD, and CAD against the US Dollar from mid-May to late July? then the three currency pairs have taken different directions.

In the next chapter, you will see the motives behind these movements, and you will learn how to analyse a country's economy through its macroeconomic data.

MACRO-DATA ANALYSIS

CHAPTER 17

∾

Now, let's analyse the economies of the two countries that make up a currency pair, trying to evaluate their strengths in order to get an indication of the movements the currency pair could make in the coming months.

Let's begin with EURUSD (table 1), first analysing the Eurozone and then the United States, which is done through the most important macroeconomic data that are released monthly or quarterly. It is very simple; you need to create tables with the main "indicators" that you will update after every release [Data 2017].

Macro-data	DEC	JAN	FEB	MAR	APR	MAY	JUN	JUL	AUG
Interest Rate	0.0%	0.0%		0.0%	0.0%		0.0%	0.0%	
Unemployment Rate	9.8%	9.8%	9.6%	9.6%	9.5%	9.5%	9.3%	9.3%	9.1%
GDP			0.5%			0.5%			0.6%
Zew	13.8	16.6	10.4	12.8	19.5	20.6	18.6	17.5	10.0
Flash PMI	54.9	55.1	55.5	56.2	56.8	57.0	57.3	56.8	57.4
CPI y/y	1.1%	1.8%	2.0%	1.5%	1.9%	1.4%	1.3%	1.3%	1.5%
Retail Sales	1.1%	-0.4%	-0.3%	-0.1%	0.7%	0.3%	0.1%	0.4%	0.5%

Table 1 - Eurozone macroeconomic data (2017)

To create the table, I used Excel but you can use any programme you like, there are also free open-source ones. Now, you would also need to create an economic data indicator for the United States as shown in table 2.

Macro-data	DEC	JAN	FEB	MAR	APR	MAY	JUN	JUL	AUG
Interest Rate	0.75		0.75	1.00		1.00	1.25	1.25	
NFP Payrolls	178K	156K	227K	235K	98K	211K	138K	222K	209K
Average Hr. Earnings	-0.1%	0.4%	0.1%	0.2%	0.2%	0.3%	0.2%	0.2%	0.3%
Unemployment Rate	4.6%	4.7%	4.8%	4.7%	4.5%	4.4%	4.3%	4.4%	4.3%
Advance GDP		1.9%			0.7%			2.6%	
ISM Manufacturing	53.2	54.7	56	57.7	57.2	54.8	54.9	57.8	56.3
CPI m/m	0.2%	0.3%	0.6%	0.1%	-0.3%	0.2%	-0.1%	0.0%	0.1%
PPI m/m	0.4%	0.3%	0.6%	0.3%	-0.1%	0.5%	0.0%	0.1%	-0.1%
Retail Sales	0.1%	0.6%	0.4%	0.1%	-0.2%	0.4%	-0.3%	-0.2%	0.6%
Building Perm	1.20M	1.21M	1.29M	1.21M	1.26M	1.23M	1.17M	1.25M	1.22M
Existing Home	5.61M	5.49M	5.69M	5.48M	5.71M	5.57M	5.62M	5.52M	5.44M

Table 2 - United States macroeconomic data (2017)

For convenience, I have only considered data from the last nine months, but you could include data from a longer period – I recommend at least the previous 18/24 months of data for good analysis.

At this point you draw conclusions from the above data, the first thing you can deduce is that the American economy continues to grow moderately, with the gross domestic product expanding at a more sustained pace in the second quarter. Labour continues to strengthen with wages growing but not by much, rather steadily every month. The unemployment rate has dropped by about half a percentage point since the beginning of the year.

Consumer price (CPI) is falling, which keeps inflation below 2% (Fed target) also because it is not affected by the energy component i.e., crude oil, which has been in a bearish trend for the last several months. Consumer spending data also declined slightly, although consumer confidence (data not shown) remained broadly unchanged.

Concerning the Eurozone, the data released confirmed Draghi's words on the growth of the Eurozone.

Gross domestic product (GDP) is expanding at a more sustained pace, increasing the final estimates for the year to 2.2%. Data regarding employment have improved, and the unemployment rate fell to 0.8% in the first eight months of the year.

The Zew grows but remains below the long-term average of 23.8 points. Consumer prices (CPI) are on the rise, even though inflation remains below the 2% target (1.5% in August). Retail Sales data improves.

From our data, you have the US economy is expanding at a moderate pace, while there are signs of major improvements in activity across the Eurozone.

Let's see other economies. You start with Australia, beginning always by building the table with the most important macroeconomic data (table 3).

Macro-data	DEC	JAN	FEB	MAR	APR	MAY	JUN	JUL	AUG
Interest Rate	1.50%		1.50%	1.50%	1.50%	1.50%	1.50%	1.50%	1.50%
Unempl. Change	39.1K	13.5K	13.5K	-6.4K	60.9K	37.4K	42.0K	14.0K	27.9K
Unemployment Rate	5.8%	5.7%	5.8%	5.9%	5.9%	5.7%	5.5%	5.6%	5.6%
GDP	-0.5%			1.1%			0.3%		
CPI q/q		0.5%			0.5%			0.2%	
Retail Sales	0.5%	0.2%	-0.1%	0.4%	-0.1%	-0.1%	1.0%	0.6%	0.3%
Building Approvals	-12.6M	7.0M	-1.2M	1.8M	8.3M	-13.4M	4.4M	-5.6M	10.9M

Table 3 - Australia macroeconomic data (2017)

The Macroeconomic data draw a favourable situation for the Australian economy with the Gross Domestic Product expanding and expected at 3% in 2017, higher than initially estimated.

Inflation is also growing and is expected at 2% in the second half of the year. Falling unemployment rate in June has reached the lowest level since March 2013 (at 5.6% in August). Consumer spending data remains weak because of lower wage growth.

Increasing exports thanks not only to China, whose growth is higher than the estimates but also to the major advanced economies that have seen the growth in potential rates. Trade Balance (data not shown), in fact, after the last two years where only negative signs have been registered, this year has seen (at least so far) exports exceed imports.

The economy of Australia is, therefore, growing even higher than the estimates, and the end of the mining boom now seems to be overcome. Only consumptions have not restarted vigorously.

Now, let's see the table with the macroeconomic data released by New Zealand (table 4).

Macro-data	DEC	JAN	FEB	MAR	APR	MAY	JUN	JUL	AUG
Interest Rate			1.75%	1.75%		1.75%	1.75%		1.75%
Unemployment Rate			5.2%			4.9%			4.8%
GDP	1.1%			0.4%			0.5%		
CPI q/q		0.4%			1.0%			0.0%	
PPI q/q			1.0%			0.8%			1.4%
Retail Sales			0.6%			1.5%			2.0%

Table 4 - New Zealand macroeconomic data (2017)

New Zealand has conflicting data. The Gross Domestic Product has grown, but by less than expected. Falling inflation because the oil and food price rises that had characterised 2017 are now missing, and (data not reported) the real estate market has slowed.

Conversely, consumer spending has risen due to strong population growth, and the employment with an unemployment rate dropped to 4.8%.

New Zealand after a stagnation period, which saw rates falling from 3.50% (April 29, 2015) to 1.75% (November 9, 2016), is trying to get out and start a growth phase, but it is still too weak.

Our last macroeconomic data analysis is Canadian economy (table 5).

Macro-data	DEC	JAN	FEB	MAR	APR	MAY	JUN	JUL	AUG
Interest Rate	0.5%	0.5%		0.5%	0.5%	0.5%		0.75%	
Unemployment Rate	6.8%	6.9%	6.8%	6.6%	6.7%	6.5%	6.6%	6.5%	6.3%
GDP m/m	-0.3%	0.4%	0.3%	0.6%	0.0%	0.5%	0.2%	0.6%	0.3%
CPI m/m	-0.4%	-0.2%	0.9%	0.2%	0.2%	0.4%	0.1%	-0.1%	0.0%
Manufacturing Sales	-0.8%	1.5%	1.3%	0.6%	-0.2%	1.0%	1.1%	1.1%	-1.8%
Retail Sales	1.4%	0.1%	-0.3%	1.7%	-0.1%	-0.2%	1.5%	-0.1%	0.7%

Table 5 - Canada macroeconomic data (2017)

Canadian economic activity has grown strongly in recent quarters. Growth in GDP in the first quarter of 2017 has increased sharply to 3.7%. Inflation (CPI) is soft for the most part because of food, electricity, and automobile prices. Consumer spending data is supported by the growing expansion of employment and an increase in wage growth and the unemployment rate in August touched the lowest since December 2008. Canada's exports have continued to recover and can be expected to keep expanding (data not shown).

Canada is in a phase of strong growth. Excluding inflation, still below the target of 2%, all other data shows a healthy economy far beyond expectations.

To sum up, you have seen that the USD bearish movement since mid-May is mainly due to a "*generalised US Dollar weakness as markets re-assess the likely pace of monetary policy normalisation in the United States.*" That stands against a favourable economic situation, with the economies of major countries often growing beyond the estimates. However, depending on the currencies against which USD is opposed, the bearish movement has developed in different ways.

NZDUSD. After the peak on July 27, 2017, the currency pair has started to decline (also because the New Zealand economy is not yet in a well-established growth). From the excess of the price, the currency pair is back below the fundamental resistance in the 0.73400 area. The Governor of the Reserve Bank of New Zealand during the August meeting stressed that "*the exchange rate remains higher than is sustainable for balanced growth in the economy and continues to dampen import prices and tradable inflation.*"

AUDUSD. Initially, the currency pair moved upwards to the highs on the strength of the gold that pushed the Australian Dollar. International tensions (particularly with North Korea) helped the gold investment, which as you will see later is directly correlated to the Australian currency, the currency pair started declining, and from the technical resistance, it went back to a correct price, below the fundamental resistance much like what happened to NZDUSD price action.

USDCAD. The currency pair has fallen sharply since May. A Canadian economy that grows at a faster pace than expected has led the Bank of Canada to raise rates twice (July 12 and September 9), and this has helped to push USDCAD even further down, reaching an area of 1.21000 (1700 pips lost in little more than four months).

Given this analysis, you can comprehend why AUDUSD remained near highs for a longer period of time, and why later it dropped less than NZDUSD (the Australian economy was stronger than New Zealand one, and gold rose from mid-July by about $ 150 an ounce). Whereas USDCAD, despite crude oil was (and still is) anchored below $ 50 a barrel, the currency pair collapsed because of the price of oil which is the strength of the Canadian economy in addition to two rate hikes by the bank of Canada (you will understand the relevance of this in Commodity Currencies in Chapter 20).

This is how to analyse the economy of a country through macroeconomic data. At first glance, it may seem complicated, but with a little practice and experience, it will get easier to do. In this type of analysis, you must always add the statements and minutes of the central banks in order to get a complete picture of what market expectations are.

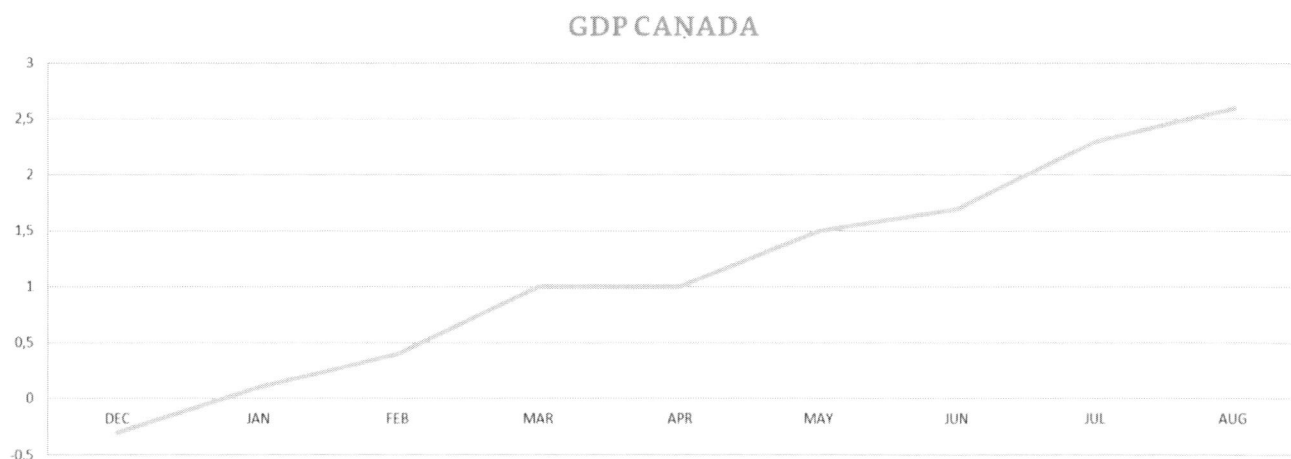

Figure 24 - GDP Canada

For example, if you look at the charts in the previous chapter, it becomes apparent that when US rates rose on March 15th and June 15th, the US dollar had not strengthened, but in fact weakened. The reason for the rate rises is mainly due to the high liquidity post QE. Expectations of the market were for something more, some other measures to absorb liquidity, that have not been present. Investors were disappointed and the Dollar was sold.

Lastly, I would add that if you want to have a representation of the data with more visual impact, you can use graphs. Here are some examples, starting with the Canadian GDP in Figure 24 above.

I added up the monthly data for better reading. As you can see, in 9 months the Canadian GDP grew by 3%, going from -0.3% in December to 2.7% in August. Below are two other examples. Figure 25, the chart of the CPI of the United States and Figure 26, the Retail Sales of the Eurozone.

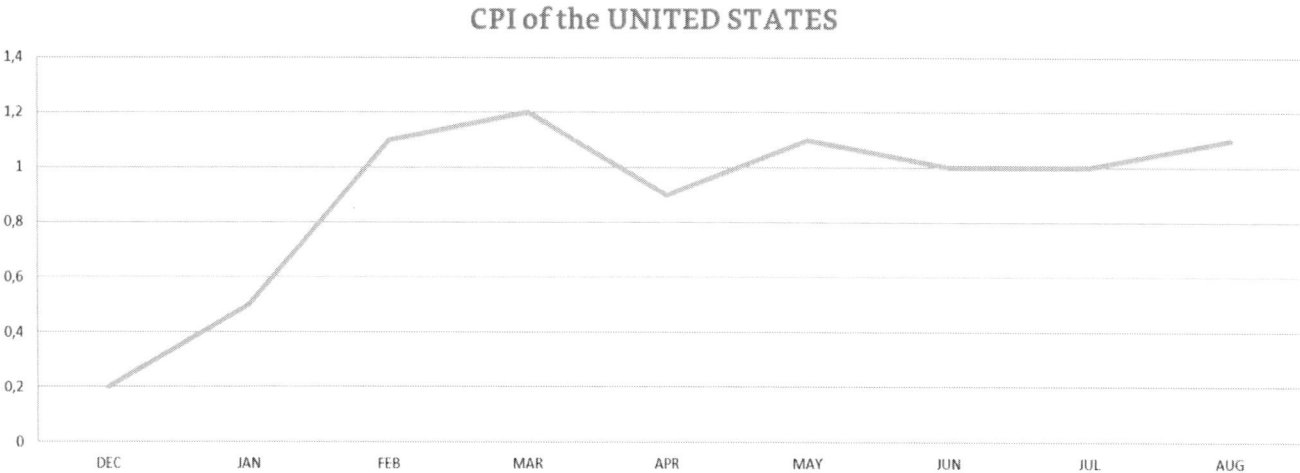

Figure 25 - CPI of the United States

Figure 26 - Retail Sales Eurozone

From the graphs above, you can easily see that from March to August, inflation in the United States has remained practically unchanged, while Eurozone consumption in the last five months has progressively increased.

Graphs are also useful for comparing the data of two or more economies, such as the Retail Sales in Figure 27, so that you check which of them has had a better trend.

Retail Sales USA and EUROZONE

Figure 27 - Retail Sales, USA and Eurozone

Graphs make it easier and faster to analyse the data of two economies that are of interest to us. Precisely, you can immediately see that up to March the American data is better than the Eurozone one, while from April to August the exact opposite happens.

However, even more, can be done. In fact, if from the data of an economy you subtract those of the other, what you get is a graph of even greater visual impact. In Figure 28 you see the Retail Sales of the United States and the Eurozone, but this time as a difference.

Retail Sales USA - EUROZONE

Figure 28 - Retail Sales, USA - Eurozone

The trend of the two data is very clear in this graph. The rise up to March, which, as already mentioned, indicates better American data than the Eurozone, and then the decline with the Eurozone data that grows more. Another example in Figure 29, with the Canadian and US Unemployment Rate.

Unemployment Rate CANADA - USA

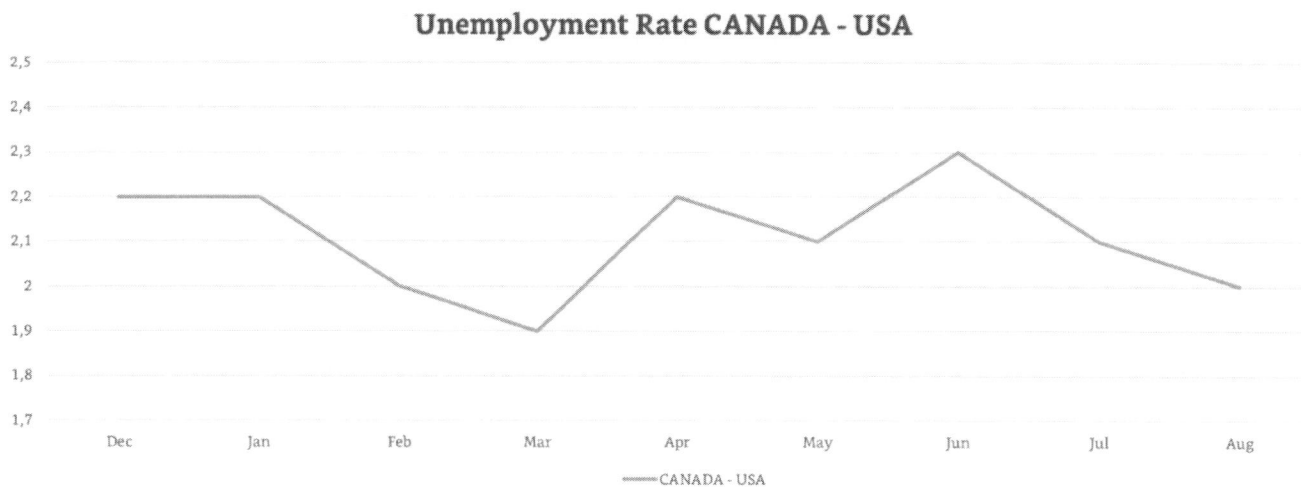

Figure 29 - Unemployment Rate, Canada - USA

Here too the trend of the two data is very clear. It is clear we see an initial drop, with the Canadian Unemployment Rate data being better than the American one, a central phase where the inverse occurs with the graph rising, and a final part where again it is the Canadian data that improves more than the American one.

GDP q/q EUROZONE - USA

Figure 30 - Gross Domestic Product, Eurozone – USA

It is all a matter of organisation of data and learning to read it in a way that is comprehensible for you. Once the data is collated it must be evaluated together with the chart of the relative currency pair. For example, let's use EURUSD.

Below, in Figures 30, 31, 32 and 33 are graphs of GDP, Unemployment rate, Manufacturing PMI and Retail Sales for the Eurozone and the US, constructed by subtracting the US data from the Eurozone data. So, if the graph of the data goes up, except for the Unemployment rate where the opposite is true, it means that the Eurozone has appreciated relative to the US. If the graph goes down, then the US has appreciated more than the Eurozone.

Unemployment rate EUROZONE - USA

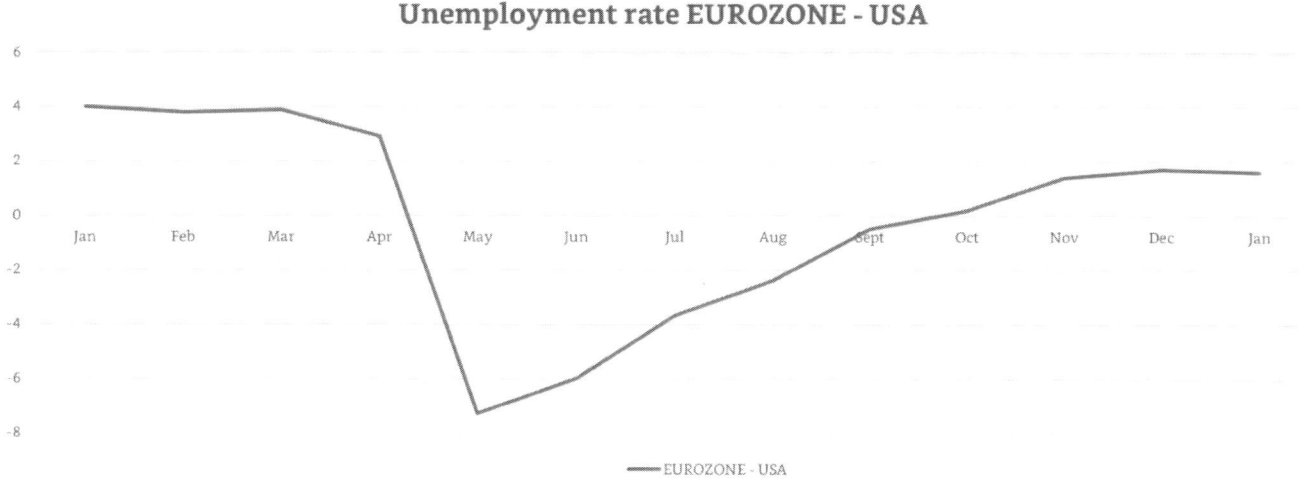

Figure 31 - Unemployment Rate, Eurozone - USA

The graph above is related to the Covid-19 unemployment rate – a unique period that affected the entire world. Notice the steep drop from April to May. However, what emerged from the graphs above and below is that in the second half of 2020, the US economy appreciated over the eurozone economy.

Manufacturing PMI EUROZONE - USA

Figure 32 - Manufacturing PMI, Eurozone - USA

In fact, the graph for GPD in Figure 30 shows a decline (although the Q4 2020 data is missing, it will be released in late January for the US and early February for the Eurozone), closely linked to manufacturing and retail sales, which have all fallen in recent months, while the one concerning unemployment rates has risen.

Figure 33 - Retail Sales, Eurozone - USA

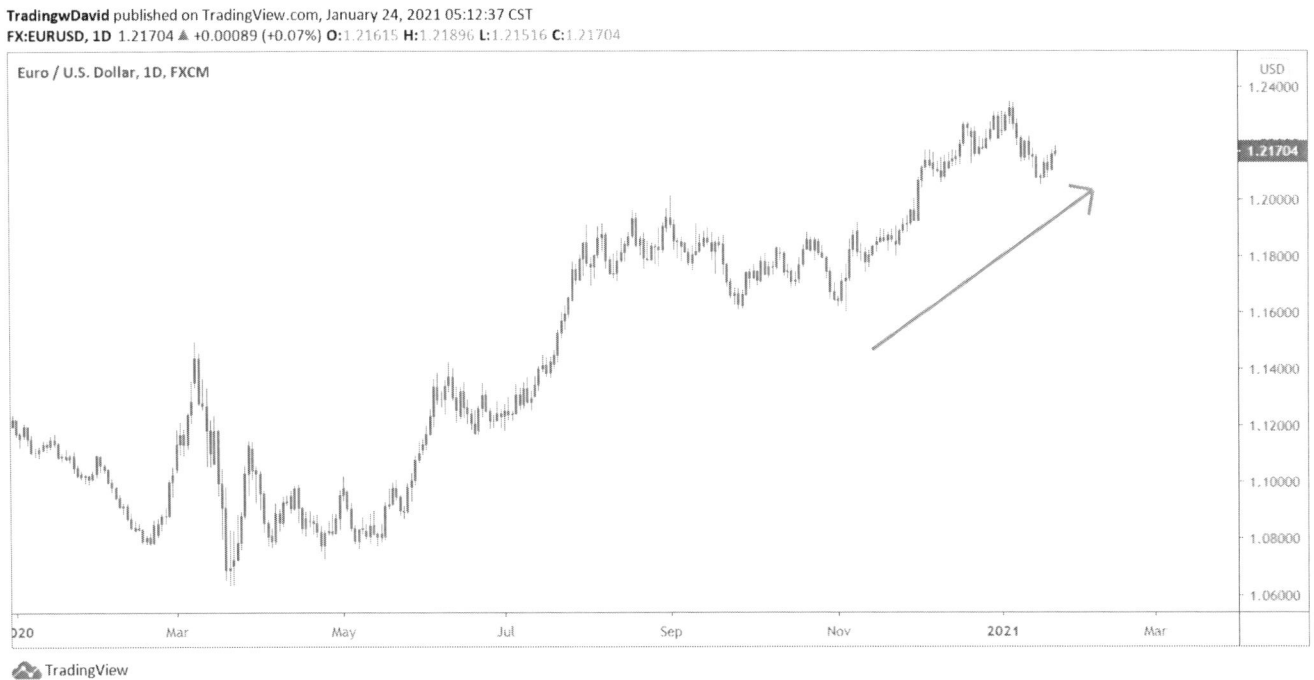

Figure 34 – EURUSD daily chart (TradingView.com)

After the "earthquake" caused by the pandemic, the US economy practically made up for what it had lost in the middle months of the year to the Eurozone economy.

Figure 34, EURUSD chart is the result that has emerged from our macroeconomic data analysis. Now, look at the chart of EURUSD to see if the trend has respected the analysis we made earlier.

The EURUSD trend is bullish since mid-May, from time to time interspersed with roughly long phases of sideways movements. This is particularly the case since the end of October and does not agree with the analysis of macroeconomic data.

Thus, it can be argued that the EURUSD exchange rate level is incorrect, it should be lower (the full analysis can be found in Chapter 30).

Important! Do not forget that this is only one part of the analysis, other aspects such as central bank policies (their forecasts), QE, socio-political events, etc. must be considered. The picture that we get at the end may well be different.

SOME COMMENTS PART 1

CHAPTER 18

~

In Chapter 15 we learnt fundamental supports and resistances, and how to analyse a currency pair through macroeconomic data. Before understanding how to combine everything through the study of some currency pairs, I want to make some awareness – mainly two points that you should include in your overall analysis of any currency pair.

Below, you can see the EURUSD daily chart (Figure 35).

Figure 35 - EURUSD daily chart (TradingView.com)

The first point, as you draw the fundamental supports and resistances, you need to acknowledge some aspects. A decision, like the interest rate cut or rise, might be known days or weeks before it happens, and it might already be priced into the market. Furthermore, you must also bear in mind the nature of that decision.

Look at the EURUSD chart, notably the two hikes in US interest rates in March and June 2017. As you can see, the currency pair, rather than decreasing as it was logical to expect, it has risen. Why? The answer is simple: it is not because the three rate hikes for the year 2017 announced by Janet Yellen, as chair of the Fed (still until February 2018), were well known months before, but because it was not in their intention to put a brake on a galloping American economy. They have been made to reduce the liquidity that has been created with Quantitative Easing (the same process will most likely see the European Union becoming the protagonist in the future).

Not only that, if you look at the day of the first interest rate hike, March 15, the EURUSD chart has also formed a tall daily green candle. In this circumstance, Investors expected some more indication from Yellen, or perhaps an intervention more capable of absorbing excess liquidity. The silence of the Fed Chair in this sense has brought disappointment among the investors who have, thus, chosen to sell dollars.

You should therefore always contemplate all the aspects, and weigh every word said or not said by the presidents of central banks because they are the main market movers in Forex, the largest currency manipulators with their decisions on monetary policy. I understand that anyone trying for the first time to read currencies in this way might view them as somewhat complicated. This was the case for me as well, besides the fact that my English at the time was not even remotely good.

Figure 36 - USDCAD daily chart (TradingView.com)

As I always say, becoming an engineer requires several years of study and practice. To become a pianist ten years of conservatory and practice every day for hours. I do not see why trading should be any different. Trading is a business and with time and diligence, the method of reading macroeconomic fundamentals of the currency market will become simple and natural.

The Second point. Looking at USDCAD (Figure 36). The same chart that you have seen two chapters earlier. The currency pair has rebounded in recent weeks from the August lows, returning to the levels of the first of two rate hikes made by the Bank of Canada.

Macroeconomic conditions have not changed from August to today (beginning of December 2017). At these levels, the US Dollar has a value too high compared with the reality of the Canadian economy. But what the analysis does not tell you is the timing of the bearish entry on USDCAD. You look at the chart a month later (Figure 37).

As you can see, USDCAD initially drops but then starts to move sideways in a range of about 230 pips, forming what in technical analysis is called a "rectangle". I know that if the initial conditions do not change, the currency pair will have to fall and return to a correct price. What I do not know is when it will.

So, the fundamental analysis gives us a background situation of a currency pair, tells us which of the two currencies is stronger, if the current price is correct or not but does not tell us when to open a position, that is, the timing of the market entry.

Figure 37 - USDCAD daily chart (TradingView.com)

Figure 38 - AUDUSD daily chart (TradingView.com)

In two other charts that you have already seen, AUDUSD (Figure 38 above) and NZDUSD (Figure 39 below), you noticed how prices can go into excess (spike) even long before returning to their correct values. Certainly, it is not enough of a reason to open a trade solely based on the rejection of price at higher level (spike).

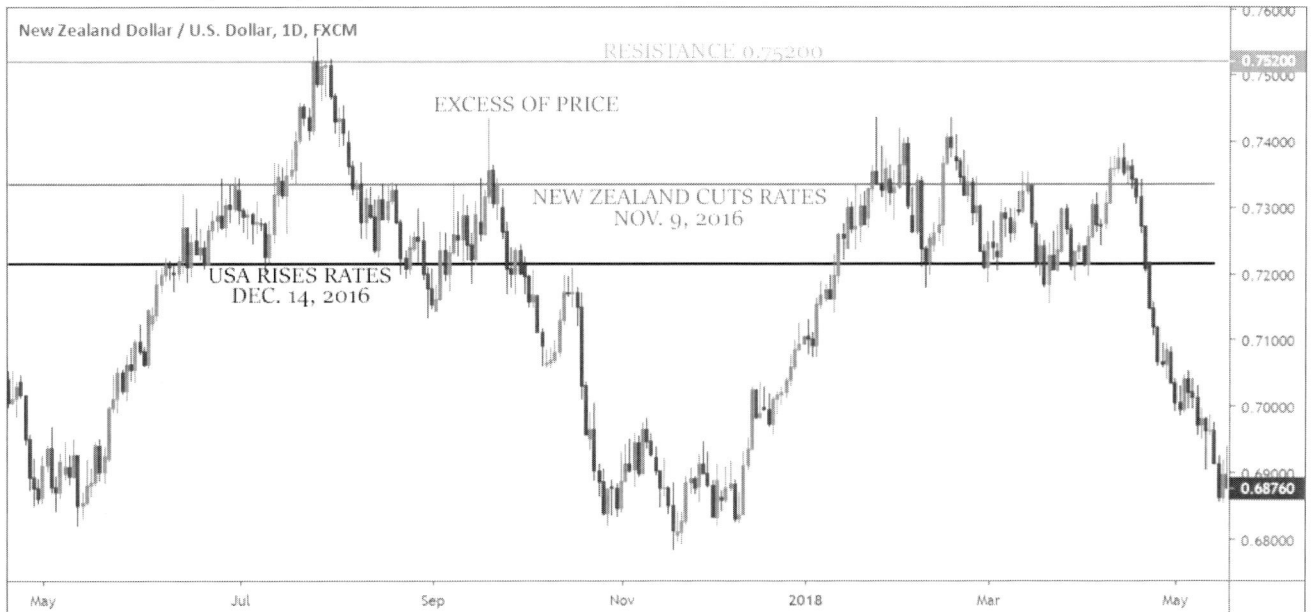

Figure 39 - NZDUSD daily chart (TradingView.com)

For the sake of clarity, I removed the lines of the rate hikes in the United States in 2017. As you can see, a greater or lesser extent, the two currency pairs have exceeded in price. The latest rate cuts in Australia and New Zealand represent significant levels beyond which you have, in fact, excesses of price.

The question then becomes, how do we know when to open a position as suggested by the fundamental analysis? Let's see that in the next chapter.

SUBJECTIVE PROBABILITY

CHAPTER 19

~

Opening a trade, just because a pattern on the chart tells you that you should, is a bad way to trade. I do not see technical analysis as the solution but as the problem. You need to identify sensitive levels for the currency pair to open your position. As I said previously, you apply subjective probability, which is, the numeric measure of chance (probability) that reflects the degree of a personal belief in the likelihood of an occurrence.

Subjective probability judgments are people's evaluations of the probability of uncertain events or outcomes. It contains no formal calculations and only reflects the subject's opinions and level of experience. It is widely believed that subjective probabilities are the foundation for common errors and biases observed in the market. That does not surprise me, given how many losing traders there are, and the ignorance (understood as lack of knowledge) that hovers around trading.

We all know who Warren Buffett is. Few people know that Buffet's decision process is an exercise in subjective probability. Buffet uses the "risk arbitrage" ("*risk arbitrage is something I have been doing for forty years now*"). And if you deepen your knowledge of the Oracle of Omaha, you can see quite clearly that Buffett's risk arbitrage estimates are subjective probabilities. You can read more about it in the book "*The Warren Buffett Portfolio – Mastering the Power of the Focus Investment Strategy*."

Well, how can you use subjective probability to find the market entry?

Let's start by saying that subjective probability differs from trader to trader. This is obvious since traders have different opinions and experiences. Without a shred of doubt, it is the experience together with the knowledge of the currency pair, which will be your best advisors. They are the ones who will give you those sensitive points that put the highest odds of success for your market entry.

Over time you need to understand how a specific currency pair behaves, the movements it makes, and how it achieves them. Your observations of these moves of when how and why will enable you to identify levels that are statistically better for opening a trade.

Yes, I understand, all this seems complicated to you. But trading is not as easy as you are led to believe by certain advertisements and websites. Know that my results come from much experience, study and practice. There is a lot of work behind the scenes to be a successful trader. You can get excellent results from Forex, maybe even better than my own, but only if you work hard and follow what I am going to teach you in this book.

You need to change your mentality and become a new person. You ought to look at Forex, and more generally trading, with different eyes. The most important thing about a trader is their mentality. The trader must have a self-starter mindset and see trading as an entrepreneurial business. Let me give an example to complete this concept. Below, you can see the EURUSD daily chart (Figure 40).

TradingwDavid published on TradingView.com, February 19, 2020 07:11:18 CST
FX:EURUSD, 1D 1.07987 ▲ +0.00074 (+0.07%) **O:** 1.07913 **H:** 1.08079 **L:** 1.07845 **C:** 1.07987

Figure 40 - EURUSD 4 daily chart (TradingView.com)

You certainly have noticed how the X.XX20 levels (i.e., 1.0920, 1.1020, 1.1120, 1.1220, etc.) for EURUSD are sensitive price levels that could be exploited, particularly for opening short-term trades (but not only).

That's just one aspect of a characteristic of EURUSD. Once you understand how the currency pair moves, and when you know it perfectly, you will no longer even need to open the chart to decide your trade.

Should be noted that the Forex world is full of these aspects, you must acquire deep knowledge of each currency pair. Below is another example. In Figure 41, you can see the

USDJPY daily chart.

Figure 41 - USDJPY daily chart (TradingView.com)

I have highlighted the first three sensitive areas above the price - you can call them Potential Reversal Zone also with the acronym PRZ. For several reasons, you intend to sell the currency pair, you just need to decide at which level to open the trade.

Under no circumstances, the last thing you want to do is open a trade at the current price just because your analysis said that the currency pair must rise or fall.

Your analysis tells you where the currency pair will go in the middle to long-term (if the conditions do not change), but in the short term, as I already said, it is always speculation that moves it.

You can easily see that the three areas have different colours. This is to help you understand better the different probabilities of the price hitting those areas and possibly reversing the trend.

Assuming the initial conditions that led you to decide to sell the currency pair have not changed, the first area (orange colour), is the one that is most likely to be hit by the price. Conversely, it is also the one with the lowest odds of seeing a price reversing the trend.

With the second area (yellow colour), the odds of the price hitting it decreases, but if this happens, the probability of seeing a trend reversal increases. The third area (green colour) is the one with a high likelihood of seeing a reversal of the trend. On the other hand, the probability of the price hitting that level is low. If the price goes beyond the green area, that's when you should review your analysis because you probably did something wrong or missed something in your analysis.

There is no rule to determine where to enter the sell order of USDJPY (or any other currency pair you are trading). Everything depends on your experience and the probability that you give to the price of reaching a certain level. If your analysis is correct, it is highly probable that the price will start a bearish movement in one of the three highlighted areas. But where would you place your sell order - which level would you choose?

In addition to your analysis, experience, and knowledge of USDJPY, it can be helpful to look at volatility. If the volatility is high, the price will probably rise above the first orange level - surely depending on the velocity, it could also overcome the second level. If, however, you have low volatility, the first level is where, most likely, you should sell the currency pair.

In this case, your approach should be: you wait until USDJPY reaches the first orange area and then you evaluate the strength of the trend, the volatility, and whether to open a full position, partially, or just keep waiting. And what about the target profit?

Figure 42 - AUDJPY daily chart (TradingView.com)

It goes without saying that you need to know when to take your profit before opening the trade – this should be in your trading plan as part of your analysis. It should be a statistically achievable profit, and just like you did with the market entry, you apply subjective probability.

The good news is and especially for the novice, that there is a way to find these sensitive areas even without a lot of experience. I am going to explain this method using the above AUDJPY daily chart (Figure 42).

On the chart, you can see I highlighted the first two sensitive areas above the price in yellow and green and the first one below it in grey.

For a beginner to find these sensitive areas, you need to use a tool called Volume Profile in the indicators section of your trading platform. What is Volume Profile?

Volume Profile is an advanced charting study that shows the traded volume amount of an asset, over a specified period at certain price levels. You immediately see the Volume Profile applied to the chart of AUDJPY (Figure 43).

Figure 43 - AUDJPY daily chart with Volume Profile (TradingView.com)

There are three different types of volume profiles that you can use in your trading. These types are not so different in what they do but rather how they are displayed on the chart.

I recommend the basic Volume Profile tool, the VPVR (Volume Profile Visible Range). It shows the amount of volume occurring at certain price levels. The Volume Profile is a study of the volume based on price; it is a bit different when compared to the horizontal volume that you see at the bottom of the chart.

Let's briefly look at the main features. Volume profile shows volume data as a histogram on the right (nothing forbids you from putting it on the left-hand side if you prefer) with different colours. The zone with yellow and blue colours is called Value Area (VA) where 70% of the volume is located in the Volume Profile. The green line high at 78.150 (VAH or Value Area High) is the highest point in the Value Area section. The green line low at 71.05 (VAL or Value Are Low) is the lowest point in the Value Area section. Usually, they are supports and resistances.

Every single bar on the histogram of the Volume Profile is called Node. You can find High Volume Nodes (HVN), points in the volume profile where there is a significantly higher volume than average, and Low Volume Nodes (LVN), points in volume profile where there is a significantly lower volume than average.

The highest volume node on the volume profile is called Point of Control (POC). It is the "gravity centre" in the chart because it is an important retest point. The price tends to come back to that level. If you take the chart of AUDJPY (Figure 44), you can see the three areas highlighted coincide with the POC and the HVN. Remember, high volume reinforces the importance of support or resistance.

Figure 44 - AUDJPY daily chart (TradingView.com)

Below, you can see the chart with the same areas highlighted and the Volume Profile added in (Figure 45).

FX:AUDJPY, 1D 73.179 ▼ −0.319 (−0.43%) O:73.498 H:73.535 L:73.075 C:73.179

Figure 45 - AUDJPY daily chart with Volume Profile (TradingView.com)

Keep in mind, if the time frame on the chart increases – suppose you trade Daily and moved to weekly charts you'll notice, the Volume Profile changes (Value Area and, most likely, the POC). The same is the case if it decreases (from monthly to daily)

This is because, if there are fewer trading days, there will also be fewer volumes and vice versa – also distributed differently. I generally use the chart with the last 9-10 months on it.

It is rare to find the Volume Profile for free on the various available platforms. To use Volume Profile in TradingView, you need a pro account or a free trial.

So far you have seen how to find sensitive areas of the price confirmed by a sharp increase in volumes. Volume Profile help traders see where to enter and exit a trade by revealing those price levels that tend to attract a currency pair players. With time you will learn to recognise these areas even without the Volume Profile on the chart.

In conclusion, no method in the world can give you a 100% chance of winning predictions; it is all a matter of probability. In the subjective probability theory, it is up to you to analyse the thesis you put together based on macroeconomic fundamentals. It differs from the technical analysis that are prompted by signals, by which, sadly, most of the times leads to a loss.

Suffice to say there's more to Volume Profile, however, what I have shown you in this chapter is sufficient to apply it to your trades. If you have doubts, curiosity, or questions, you can contact me via e-mail, social networks, or through my website.

In the next chapter, you are going to get to know better the Safe-Haven currencies.

SAFE-HAVEN CURRENCIES

CHAPTER 20

∾

When you trade currencies, you need to be very clear about all the strong points the currency pairs possess, but you also need to realise what you need to keep under control. Strategically, it is necessary to know what might put you in trouble, and what to do if and when this happens. For example, closing a trade even though it has not reached the stop-loss or target.

When there is fear, there is emotion. Financial markets are full of emotions. To classify feelings is when there is fear in the Forex market – thus you emotionally trade CHF and JPY, the so-called "Safe-Haven Currencies." You also must take care of the psychological aspect because, in trading, there are machines (algos), but there are also human beings. And in the end, it all comes down to psychology, and when there is fear the CHF and JPY are bought.

Once you sense panic in the market, you start by trying to read the emotions associated with it – analyse the relationships and improve upon them by taking the best scenarios on the chart because they are the ones that can cause large movements. Then there is the technical aspect which comes in Chapter 13 – and you must always remember that no trader is immune to these emotional difficulties hence why everyone falls back to these two currencies.

Now, you have to ask yourself some questions: do I buy Yen? but against which currency? In what moment? Does the Swiss Franc have positive components? When is it wise to put it in the portfolio and when not?

Some aspects of CHF are quite particular. Besides being a safe-haven currency, its oscillation also brings benefits or disadvantages for its own economy, considering that Switzerland is an exporting country.

The first step, to always keep always in mind, is that since Switzerland is an export-led economy, a Swiss Franc that is too strong will generate a lot of problems for their exports. In fact, the Swiss National Bank is not very happy to see EURCHF below 1.10. That is one aspect, however, when compared with all the rest of other currencies, it is inferior in importance, or better said, is considered inferior in strength.

If for example, the ECB is using only 5% for the QE, it means that the ECB can use liquidity higher than the European GDP. From this, you can understand that the force of a central bank like the ECB is superior to the will of a small nation. Crucial to keep in mind that you should always be clear about the pros and cons of each economy.

You can use CHF against EUR because it has a point in its favour. It is a currency pair that does not move much in terms of volatility compared to the other currency pairs, and this puts you in a position to see it work more comfortably.

Moreover, you cannot look at another currency pair with CHF, for example USDCHF, in the same way as EURCHF because there is a different basic analysis. It is true, that you have CHF (safe haven currency) on both the currency pairs, but there is also a change in conditions. On the one hand, there is the Euro and the Eurozone, which have a very close economic relationship with Switzerland, and for this reason, it is difficult for the EURCHF to move strongly.

On the other hand, you have USDCHF that suffers more than any other currency pairs because there is no relationship between the Swiss and the US economy strong enough to control the exchange rate. So, it becomes a currency pair that suffers the effects of the stronger currency, thereby, it is the pair where there is much more of interest.

You shall go behind the scenes of the two economies and of the two currencies that make up the currency pair. Sometimes they can be fairly complicated speeches, but this will allow you to have a broader view not only within Forex but all the financial markets as well.

As in commodity spread trading, in which you have to analyse the two legs that make up the spread, here you have to examine the two economies that make up the currency pair. If the relationship between the different economies is closely interconnected, the greater the force applied to the control.

In summary, EURCHF is very controlled because very important oscillations could undermine the Swiss exports, which would put Switzerland in great difficulty. While on USDCHF, fluctuations are much larger. So, if you have to move in order to protect your portfolio, it is much easier to do it on EURCHF where you have more "control." USDCHF instead undergoes more the "mathematical" differences that are created inside the Forex.

EURCHF is slightly anticipatory of EURUSD for its variables of coverage. There is a very close movement between EURUSD and EURCHF, especially in certain situations. When you arrive at important points of EURCHF, this can determine what might happen to EURUSD, even though this aspect is also slightly dictated by experience. Very often, you use USDCHF as a "stepchild" and opposite to the EURUSD. However, it is not a relationship that always remains unchanged and in all market moments.

EURCHF is a bit more controllable than the Yen because a movement of 300/400 pips, EURCHF does it in months. EURJPY or USDJPY can also do it in a couple of days, especially when there is a hint of a crisis. That does not mean you cannot cover yourself by buying Yen against the Euros, US Dollar or another currency. You just need to be a little more vigilant and remain more often in front of the monitor to follow the development of the currency pair.

Numerous factors are responsible for creating the dynamics that move the Japanese Yen during periods of risk aversion. While some of these factors make sense from a fundamental perspective, others are simply speculative. One wonders, how is it possible, that the market points to investing in the currency of a country that turns out to be the most indebted in the world (based on the debt/GDP ratio)?

Japan has always been a large exporter and has continually exported significantly more goods and services than it imports. The result has been decades of current account surpluses. Therefore, its currency is more in demand than sold. Not only this, for the 24th consecutive year, Japan was confirmed in 2017 as the largest creditor on the planet for assets invested outside its national territory.

Many of these investments tend to get back in times of risk, due to the inverse process of the so-called "carry trade." With the carry trade (you will learn it in Chapter 25) the market tends to borrow in the currencies of economies with low-interest rates, investing in currencies of economies at higher rates.

When financial, economic, or political tensions explode, however, as these ultimates are at greater risk, the aim is to disinvest and reconvert the liquidity obtained in the initial currency. For this reason, when there is fear, there is risk aversion, JPY tends to be bought more than sold, becoming, in fact, a safe-haven currency just like CHF (even though the dynamics are different).

In trading, there is an index that is widely used because of its nature, the VIX index. It is a measure of the implied volatility of the S&P 500 Index calculated through a weighted average of the volatility priced into its options. It represents the market's expectations of volatility over the next 30 days.

The main characteristic of the VIX Index is the inverse correlation with the trend of stock prices of the S&P500. This characteristic, which has earned it the name "fear index" is because as the index rises, the "fear" in the markets substantially increases, up to the level of "panic selling" the point at which the VIX index reaches extreme price peaks.

Let me show you graphically the relationship between fear in the markets and safe-haven currencies. Let's start with the chart of EURCHF, in black, with the VIX Index, in red (Figure 46).

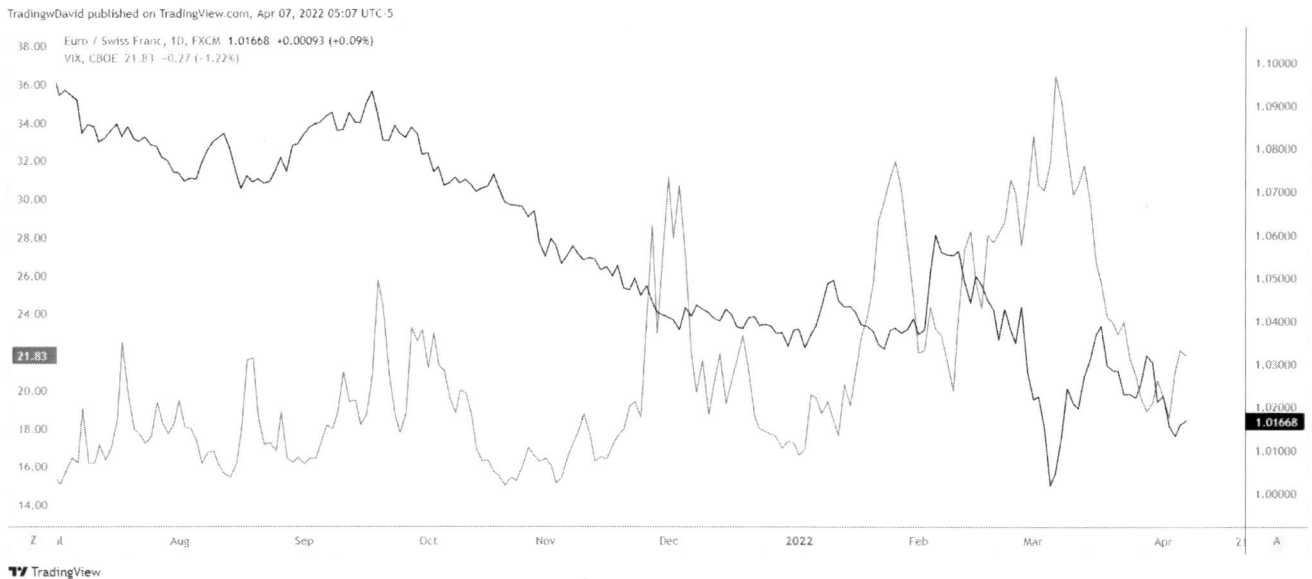

Figure 46 - EURCHF and VIX Index (TradingView)

When the VIX Index is low or falling, the currency pair moves would follow dynamics such as speculation and central banks' decisions. On the other hand, when the VIX Index rises, especially above 30, the EURCHF would fall, sometimes as heavily as it did in early 2022.

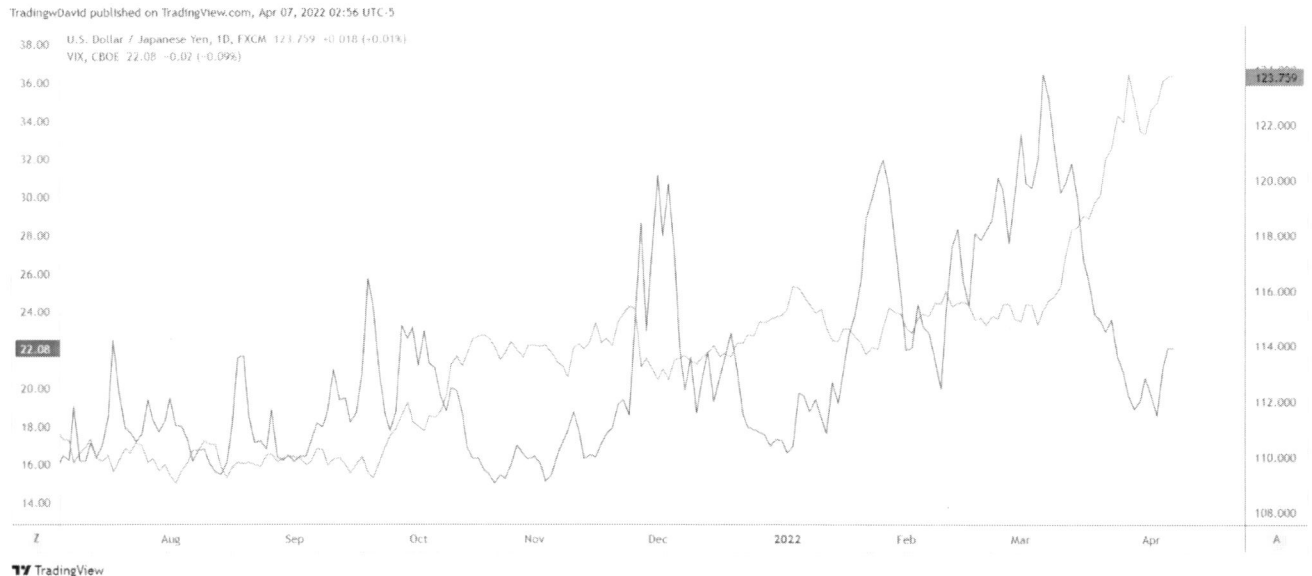

Figure 47 - USDJPY and VIX Index (TradingView)

In Figure 47 above, you can see the chart of USDJPY (in green) with the VIX Index (in red). Compared to the EURCHF chart, the movements are less pronounced and, most importantly, in early 2022, the currency pair does not go down but has a strong bullish movement. You will see the reason for this later.

Because of its status as a strong currency, the US dollar is also seen as a safe-haven currency when black clouds are gathering over the markets. In Figure 48 you can see the chart of EURUSD (in blue) with the VIX Index (in red).

Figure 48 - EURUSD and VIX Index (TradingView)

The inverse correlation between EURUSD and the VIX Index is very clear, especially when the "fear index" rises.

Trading cannot be reduced to an algorithm. Mine is not a criticism of automated trading, I just want to say that when there is fear in the financial markets, especially when you see Wall Street collapse, it is not wise to automatically buy CHF, JPY, not even USD. You must always analyse the situation, understand well what is happening. Otherwise, you could end up selling USDJPY and see the currency pair rise sharply.

The Yen, besides being a safe-haven currency, is used, as mentioned earlier, for carry trade. Institutional investors and hedge funds with the prospect of numerous Federal Reserve rate hikes during the year, have begun to buy USDJPY by taking advantage of the yield differential. This is the reason why, despite the sharp rise in the VIX Index, the USDJPY has not fallen but rather has risen by over 9% in just over three weeks.

In this regard, I show you one more chart. In Figure 49 you can see the chart of AUDJPY (in black) again with the VIX Index. Many traders use this currency pair as a thermometer of the financial markets and, looking at the chart, it is understandable why, given the strong inverse correlation with the VIX Index.

However, in February 2022, during the VIX Index surge, this correlation was lost, with the currency pair beginning a sharp rise. Again, there is a good reason for this. With the outbreak of war in Ukraine, you have seen a strong rise in many commodity prices. This rise has benefited the commodity currencies (you will see in the next chapter), with especially AUD and NZD strengthening against all major currencies.

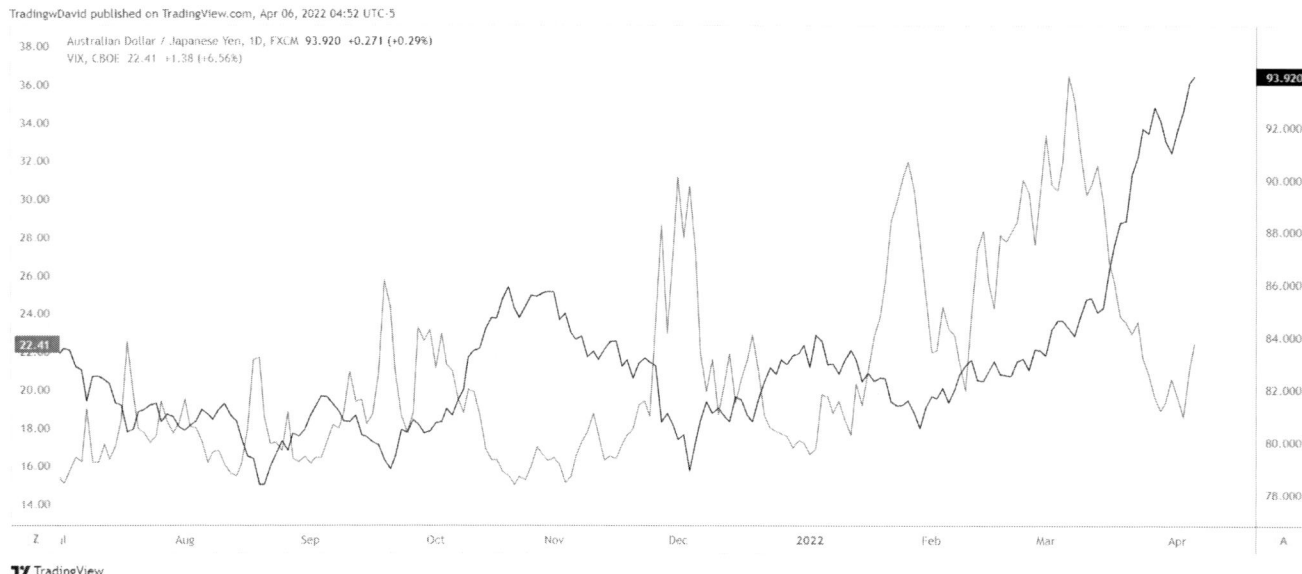

Figure 49 - AUDJPY and VIX Index (TradingView)

I conclude this chapter by saying, it is important to have CHF in your portfolio but should always be bought at certain levels. This allows you to cover not only the other Forex operations but also your whole portfolio. Alternatively, you can use JPY, but you must always keep in mind that while EURCHF is easily controllable thanks to the economic relationship between the Eurozone and Switzerland, Yen is more volatile and requires a greater presence in front of the monitor.

Evaluate each situation well, events could also push investors to sell the Swiss franc and especially the Yen. Do not underestimate the fact that both are currencies used in carry trade (even though this concept is not clear to you right now). You should never be in a hurry to open a trade and take anything for granted. Do not be superficial in your analysis but take a 360-degree view of what is happening in the world, not just in trading.

COMMODITY CURRENCIES

CHAPTER 21

~

The term "Commodity Currencies" refers to the currencies of the countries which are heavily dependent on the export of certain raw materials, such as crude oil, precious metals, and agricultural products. There are several commodity currencies; the most traded in the Forex market are the Canadian Dollar, Australian Dollar, and New Zealand Dollar.

Unlike other countries that export commodities, exports of these countries are an essential part of their Gross Domestic Product (GDP) annually. As such, fluctuations in value or quantity of goods exported to these countries will have a more significant impact on their currencies. Typically, then, if the price of the raw material grows, the currency of a great exporter country will appreciate more than the other currencies. However, this should be considered with caution.

Commodity currencies depict a more complex interpretation than simply a direct market linked to the price of an underlying asset. The performance of a commodity currency can be influenced by several independent factors outside the commodities dynamics, especially in the short-term. One of these is the differential that may form between interest rates of these countries.

For example, those of Australia (and New Zealand) with those of Japan: in general, the capital will tend to move where the rates, and then the remuneration, are higher. It involves an appreciation of the country's currency exchange rate that is attracting more capital.

Not surprisingly one of the most currency pairs exploited by traders is precisely AUDJPY, which, like NZDJPY, is a very beaten path from the carry trade, the speculative strategy that exploits the disparity between the cost of borrowing money where it costs less and investing it where it will make more. You will see more about the carry trade in chapter 25.

AUD. Australia is the world's second-largest gold producer, after South Africa. The gold exports make up a large percentage of the GDP of the country, so any changes in gold prices will have a significant impact on the GDP of Australia and the value of its currency.

In the case in which the production of gold was to diminish, this could also cause, a repercussion, a potential weakening of the Australian Dollar. The connection between the Australian Dollar and the value of gold is used as an important indicator for the currency pair AUDUSD.

In the daily chart below, you can see a comparison of the gold futures contract and AUDUSD (Figure 50).

Figure 50 - Correlation between AUDUSD and Gold (TradingView.com)

Australia is not only a great producer of gold but is also a major exporter of crude oil and copper – the latter directly connected with China. To a lesser extent, it also exports meat and grains.

So, you can see explicitly how Australia is a major exporter of commodities, particularly to China. And for this reason, the Chinese economy is connected to the Australian Dollar.

NZD. The basket of currency pairs in Forex is very wide. There are, however, very liquid currencies, which are the most traded, and some others which are less important from this point of view. The currency of New Zealand is inserted into the basket of the Majors, but for trading and the importance that it has on the Forex market, it cannot be treated like all the other Majors.

If EURUSD makes certain percentage movements, for a currency pair inside the New Zealand Dollar, this percentage is much higher, and it has far more significant fluctuations.

It means, the liquidity that NZD moves is much smaller and therefore much more manoeuvrable. And what is much more manoeuvrable is much less controllable for traders. As a result, it is a very dangerous currency, far more speculative, and in many ways comparable to Exotics.

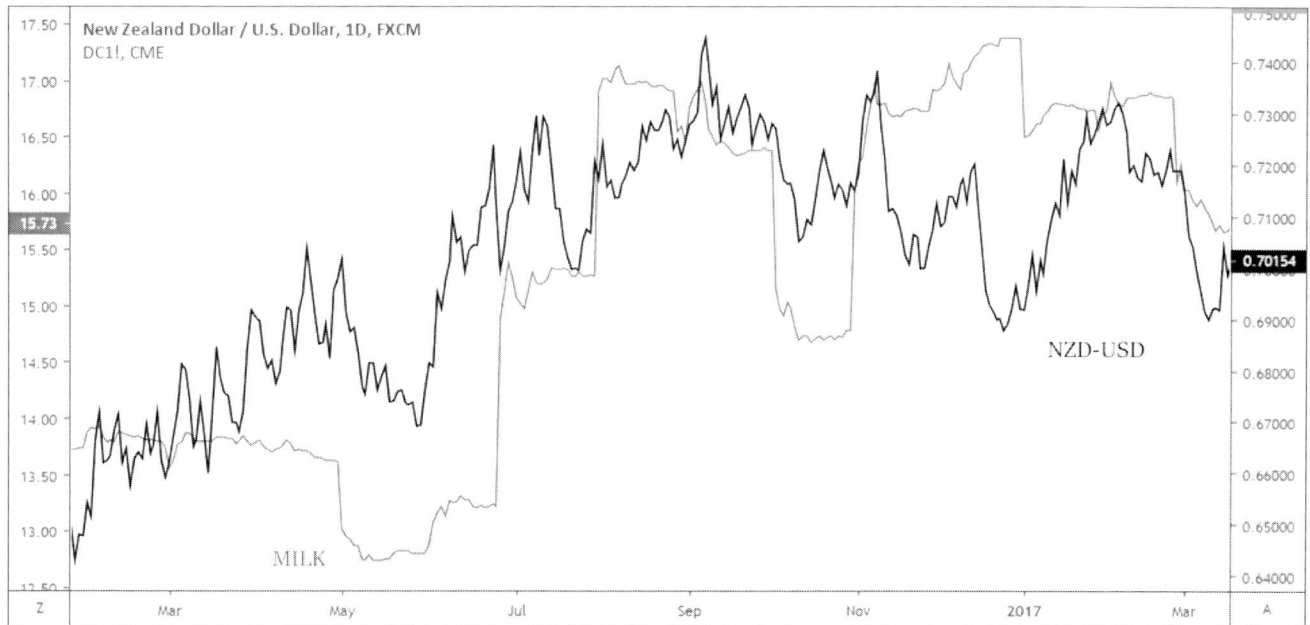

Figure 51 - Correlation NZDUSD and Milk (TradingView.com)

You got to use this currency sparingly, and in any case only if you have the option to keep it under control and with relatively small investment percentages.

Exports for New Zealand relate to commodities such as timber, dairy, and meat products. The various commodity indices have proved their value in the long-term as indicators of the value of the New Zealand Dollar.

In the daily chart in Figure 51 above, you can see the correlation between the Milk futures contract and NZDUSD.

CAD. Canada is oil-related since it is a large producer (is among the top 5 countries in the world, although it is not part of OPEC), and is a major exporter and therefore oil is very important for its economy.

The more the price of oil rise, the more the Canadian economy will improve, and consequently, its currency will too, hence it will get more revenue and greater profits. Canada exports oil, above all, to the United States (about two-thirds of exports). So, if the price of oil increases, the value of USDCAD decreases.

Canada is not only a major oil exporter, but another commodity also that is the object of considerable export is aluminium. Canada has also had exponential growth in exports of other metals including zinc, copper and nickel.

In the chart in Figure 52, you can see the inverse correlation between the Crude Oil futures contract and USDCAD. Here I want to make an important observation. As you can see, not always the currency pair and oil movements are in opposite directions.

FX:USDCAD, 1D 1.30315 ▲ +0.00053 (+0.04%) O:1.30327 H:1.30429 L:1.30214 C:1.30315

Figure 52 - Inverse correlation USDCAD and Crude Oil (TradingView.com)

That is because if you put the CAD, which is a strong currency, near to an even stronger currency such as USD, the chance of a movement will be to the advantage of the stronger one, in this case (and at this moment, the year 2017) the US Dollar.

This concept, I would say is almost imperative, it is the basis of how you have to treat Forex. You must look at a currency pair not as a single price, but as a clash between two economies. In this way, you can realise that putting CAD against USD or NZD is not quite the same thing.

You, therefore, must be careful which currency and which economy, you position your trade against (AUD, NZD, CAD). If you put a strong currency, say AUD against an even stronger currency such as USD, the strength of the US Dollar will cancel the benefits of AUD in case of an increase in commodity prices. As already said, the decisions of the Fed and some macroeconomic data have a greater impact than the actual commodity strength per se.

On the other hand, if you compare AUD with a weaker currency (thus with an economy), the situation is more uncertain, and a rise of some commodity prices may impart new vigour to the Australian Dollar.

In the next chapter, you are going to see how you can analyse a currency pair using everything you have learnt thus far.

ANALYSIS OF A CURRENCY PAIR

CHAPTER 22

~

In this chapter, you will learn how to analyse a currency pair on the basis of everything you have seen in the previous pages of this book. You are going to analyse a couple of currency pairs, so that you have a correct basic view of the economies of the two countries in question.

Let's start with GBPUSD. First, let's check out the chart, which you can see below with all the most important levels (Figure 53).

Figure 53 - GBPUSD daily chart (TradingView.com)

On June 23, 2016, with the "Brexit" referendum, the United Kingdom left the European Union, with the consequent collapse of the Pound in the following weeks.

On December 14, 2016, the United States increased interest rates by 25 basis points. Initially, macro resistance held up well, with GBPUSD falling and remaining below this level. Then the currency pair began a bullish trend.

On 2 November 2017, the United Kingdom increased the interest rates by 25 basis points to 0.50%, thus creating new macroeconomic support at 1.32500.

These are the most important macroeconomic levels. At the "technical" level, you can see static support at 1.34500, and the first resistance that the uptrend will meet at 1.41000.

Surely, the first thing you should always do is to take the chart and highlight the key levels, both macroeconomic and those deriving from the technical analysis, for the present time, and for an anticipated move, you should also highlight the zones indicated by the subjective probability.

The next step is to divide the pros and cons of the economies that make up the currency pair. Let's start with the United Kingdom.

PROS:

- Good jobs data with an increase in wages

CONS:

- Brexit (uncertainty and high inflation)
- Prime Minister Theresa May does not have a majority in Parliament
- Security (terrorist attacks)

The United Kingdom is experiencing a moment of uncertainty, both for what will be the effects of Brexit (it will enter into force in March 2019), and politics, with Prime Minister Theresa May who does not have a majority and has been defeated in Parliament several times.

Now, let's apply the same analysis to the United States, even though you have already known it, and it has not changed much over time.

PROS:

- Domestic consumption-based economy
- Currency used for international trade
- Good data regarding employment
- Tax cuts
- Three projected interest rate hikes in 2018

CONS:

- Donald Trump (Russiagate, loss of popularity, protectionist policy)
- International policy (North Korea)
- Problems with budget deficit

The United States is continuing in economic growth, with three expected rate hikes in 2018. The only uncertainty comes from Trump and his policy.

And the second step to take is to divide each economy those that are the pros and cons. We begin with a macroeconomic analysis, starting from the United Kingdom whose main macroeconomic data are reported in table 6.

Macro-data	APR	MAY	JUN	JUL	AUG	SEP	OCT	NOV	DEC
Interest Rate		0.25%	0.25%		0.25%	0.25%		0.50%	0.50%
Unemployment Rate	4.7%	4.6%	4.6%	4.5%	4.4%	4.3%	4.3%	4.3%	4.3%
Av. Earn.	2.3%	2.4%	2.1%	1.8%	2.1%	2.1%	2.2%	2.2%	2.5%
GDP	0.3%			0.3%			0.4%		
Manuf. PMI	54.2	57.3	56.7	54.3	55.1	56.9	55.9	56.3	58.2
CPI m/m	2.3%	2.7%	2.9%	2.6%	2.6%	2.9%	3.0%	3.0%	3.1%
Retail Sales	-1.8%	2.3%	-1.2%	0.6%	0.3%	1.0%	-0.8%	0.3%	1.1%
Constr. PMI	52.2	53.1	56.0	54.8	51.9	51.1	48.1	50.8	53.1
Service PMI	55.0	55.8	53.8	53.4	53.8	53.2	53.6	55.6	53.8

Table 6 - Great Britain macroeconomic data (2017)

Now, let's see the most important macroeconomic data of the United States (table 7).

Macro-data	APR	MAY	JUN	JUL	AUG	SEP	OCT	NOV	DEC
Interest Rate	0.75		0.75	1.00		1.00	1.25	1.25	

NFP Payrolls	178K	156K	227K	235K	98K	211K	138K	222K	209K
Average Hr. Earnings	-0.1%	0.4%	0.1%	0.2%	0.2%	0.3%	0.2%	0.2%	0.3%
Unemployment Rate	4.6%	4.7%	4.8%	4.7%	4.5%	4.4%	4.3%	4.4%	4.3%
Advance GDP		1.9%			0.7%			2.6%	
ISM Manufacturing	53.2	54.7	56	57.7	57.2	54.8	54.9	57.8	56.3
CPI m/m	0.2%	0.3%	0.6%	0.1%	-0.3%	0.2%	-0.1%	0.0%	0.1%
PPI m/m	0.4%	0.3%	0.6%	0.3%	-0.1%	0.5%	0.0%	0.1%	-0.1%
Retail Sales	0.1%	0.6%	0.4%	0.1%	-0.2%	0.4%	-0.3%	-0.2%	0.6%
Building Perm	1.20M	1.21M	1.29M	1.21M	1.26M	1.23M	1.17M	1.25M	1.22M
Existing Home	5.61M	5.49M	5.69M	5.48M	5.71M	5.57M	5.62M	5.52M	5.44M

Table 7 - United States macroeconomic data (2017)

From the two tables above with the most important macroeconomic data, you can see how those of the United Kingdom are conflicting. GDP had modest growth in 2017. The increase in import prices, due to the depreciation of the Pound Sterling after Brexit, pushed inflation beyond the target of 2% to 3.1% in November.

On the other hand, labour data are positive, with the unemployment rate falling to 4.3% in November and with recovery in the second half of the year of wage growth.

When analysing the data for the United States, there has been a continuous improvement in employment; the unemployment rate fell to 4.1%. However, new jobs are not accompanied by a sustained increase in wages.

Consumption and inflation are also rising, even though the latter remains below the 2% (but not by much) with a target of 1.7%.

Therefrom, the third step you have to take is to analyse the two economies through macroeconomic data. I strongly advise you to use data of the last 18/24 months for a more accurate analysis.

To complete the analysis, you got to read the statements and minutes released by the two Central Banks, BoE and the Fed. I also proceed with the United Kingdom. Below you can read the <u>main steps</u> of the last Monetary Policy Summary and Minutes.

"*GDP grew modestly over the next few years, at a pace just above its reduced rate of potential. Consumption growth remained sluggish in the near-term before rising, in line with household incomes. Global growth has remained strong. Domestically, some activity indicators suggest GDP growth in Q4 might be slightly softer than in Q3.*

Net trade was bolstered by the strong global expansion and the past depreciation of Sterling. Business investment, while affected by uncertainties around Brexit, was projected to continue to grow at a modest pace.

Unemployment was expected to remain low throughout the three-year forecast period, and domestic inflationary pressures were projected to pick up gradually as remaining spare capacity was absorbed and wage growth recovered.

Developments regarding the United Kingdom's withdrawal from the European Union – and in particular the reaction of households, businesses and asset prices to them – remain the most significant influence on, and source of uncertainty about, the economic outlook."

As for the United States, the main steps from the last statement issued by the FOMC.

"*The labour-market has continued to strengthen and that economic activity has been rising at a solid rate. Averaging through hurricane-related fluctuations, job gains have been solid, and the unemployment rate declined further.*

Household spending has been expanding at a moderate rate. On a 12-month basis, both overall inflation and inflation for items other than food and energy have declined this year and are running below 2 per cent.

The Committee continues to expect that, with gradual adjustments in the stance of monetary policy, economic activity will expand at a moderate pace and labour-market conditions will remain strong."

Finally, the fourth and last step you have to take to complete the analysis of a currency pair is to read the last Statement and Minutes of each Central Bank, and highlight the most significant steps, just as we did above.

Now you have a complete view of GBPUSD, which means you can draw your conclusions on the basis of which you will make your decisions.

The United Kingdom is experiencing a period of uncertainty after the referendum that has stated the exit from the European Union, and this was reflected in the Pound Sterling as well. This uncertainty, which is also political, concerning Prime Minister Theresa May is due to the fact that she no longer held a majority in Parliament after the last elections took place on June 8, 2017.

Macroeconomic data depict a low-growth English economy, with GDP in decline compared with the previous years. Inflation has jumped over 3% for the devaluation of the Pound Sterling. The Bank of England raised interest rates by 25 basis points in November 2017, also with the aim of curbing inflation.

On the other hand, employment data improved, with the unemployment rate declining by 0.5% in 2017 to 4.3%; data that has been accompanied in the second half of the year by a recovery in wages.

I went to see the pre-Brexit macroeconomic data (not shown), and it has only gotten better in terms of employment (in June 2016 the unemployment rate was at 5%). Retail sales remained almost unchanged, while, as mentioned, GDP declined.

The United States, on the other hand, continues to expand at a moderate pace, with labour data remaining strong, and a continuously falling unemployment rate at 4.1%, although a sustained increase in wages does not yet accompany it. There is, however, an increase in consumer spending.

Inflation is on the rise, and at the end of 2017, after the three rate hikes, it was at 1.7%, just below the 2% target. GDP is growing beyond the estimates that have been revised upwards in the last Economic Projection at 2.5% for both 2017 and 2018. Three rate hikes are confirmed for 2018.

In conclusion: the strong rise of speculative origin for GBPUSD, is not reflected in macroeconomic analysis. The American economy remains stronger than the English one and with fewer uncertainties. However, I consider it very likely that the Dollar will continue to depreciate, due to the protectionist policy that Trump intends to adopt.

From here, rather than looking for a level where to open short positions, I would open a bullish short-term trade on the Pound Sterling which, when it moves, has no problem doing it even for 200-300 pips. In this way, I try to exploit a probable weakening of the Dollar. However, in the medium to long-term, GBPUSD is expected to fall.

As you can see, a correct analysis from all points of view can also lead you to open a short-term trade against what the fundamental analysis says.

Let's move on with another currency pair, EURAUD. As a first step, replicating the same procedure seen with GBPUSD, let us take a look at the chart, which I have highlighted with the most important levels (Figure 54).

FX:EURAUD, 1D 1.66131 ▲ +0.00480 (+0.29%) O:1.65651 H:1.67870 L:1.65319 C:1.66131

Figure 54 - EURAUD daily chart (TradingView.com)

On August 2, 2016, the Royal Bank of Australia cut interest rates by 25 basis points, but despite this, for several months the currency pair moved below this level. This is due to the strong liquidity injection of the ECB, which enabled the devalue the Euro.

It is no coincidence that from the 26th of July 2017, the day when for the first time Mario Draghi, ECB chairman, talked about the possible termination of QE by the end of the year, the Euro started to rise against all the other currencies, including the Australian Dollar.

Indeed, EURAUD returned above the macroeconomic level created by the rates cut of the Reserve Bank of Australia, which, from that moment on, it became strong support. The currency pair continued to rise by breaking the resistance (now support) in the 1.52000 area, and just a couple of days before writing this chapter, it was tested.

EURAUD has different dynamics to consider, but let's proceed in the same manner as we did before. The next step is to divide the pros and cons of each economy that makes up the currency pair. Starting with the Eurozone.

PROS:

- Good data regarding employment
- GDP revised up at 2.4% this year
- The end of QE (in a soft way)

CONS:

- Immigration
- Security (terrorist attacks)
- Several political elections (in particular Italy, Hungary and Poland)
- Different economies inside
- Low Inflation

For the Eurozone, the end of Quantitative Easing should lead to an appreciation of the Euro. Added to this is an economy that grows with GDP revised upwards this year. There are still differences between the countries within it that show structural problems. There is always a constant danger of terrorist attacks. In 2018 there will be several political elections.

Now we lay out the same thing for Australia.

PROS:

- Growth in GDP and is expected to be 2.8% this year (a bit lower than 3% of some months before but still over the initial 1.8%)
- Good data regarding employment

CONS:

- Moderate consumptions
- Exports-based economy. It depends on other economies (China) and the prices of commodities
- An appreciating exchange rate would complicate growth

Australia is showing signs of recovery with a GDP higher than initial estimates and excellent data on employment. The low consumption still does not strongly stimulate growth. The economy is always based on commodities and commercial relations with China.

A weak Dollar would favour an increase in commodity prices but, at the same time, would strengthen the currency pair AUDUSD, complicating growth.

Now, we look at the main macroeconomic data of the two economies. You can find in the table below those relating to the Eurozone (table 8).

Macro-data	APR	MAY	JUN	JUL	AUG	SEP	OCT	NOV	DEC
Interest Rate	0.0%		0.0%	0.0%		0.0%	0.0%		0.0%

Unemployment Rate	9.5%	9.5%	9.3%	9.3%	9.1%	9.1%	9.1%	8.9%	8.8%
GDP		0.5%			0.6%			0.6%	
Zew	19.5	20.6	18.6	17.5	10.0	17.0	17.6	18.7	17.4
Flash PMI	56.8	57.0	57.3	56.8	57.4	58.2	58.6	60.0	60.6
CPI y/y	1.9%	1.4%	1.3%	1.3%	1.5%	1.5%	1.4%	1.5%	
Retail Sales	0.7%	0.3%	0.1%	0.4%	0.5%	-0.3%	-0.5%	0.7%	-1.1%

Table 8 - Eurozone macroeconomic data (2017)

Below, the main Australian macroeconomic data (table 9).

Macro-data	APR	MAY	JUN	JUL	AUG	SEP	OCT	NOV	DEC
Interest Rate	1.50%	1.50%	1.50%	1.50%	1.50%	1.50%	1.50%	1.50%	1.50%
Unempl. Change	60.9K	37.4K	42.0K	14.0K	27.9K	54.2K	19.8K	3.7K	61.6K
Unemployment Rate	5.9%	5.7%	5.5%	5.6%	5.6%	5.6%	5.5%	5.4%	5.4%
GDP			0.3%			0.8%			0.6%
CPI q/q	0.5%			0.2%			0.6%		
Retail Sales	-0.1%	-0.1%	1.0%	0.6%	0.3%	0.0%	-0.6%	0.0%	0.5%
Building Approvals	8.3%	-13.4%	4.4%	-5.6%	10.9%	-1.7%	0.4%	1.5%	0.9%

Table 9 - Australia macroeconomic data (2017)

From the two tables above, you can see that the Eurozone data show an improvement but it is still slow. Good data regarding employment, with the unemployment rate falling by 1% in 2017. Retail sales, however, has practically remained steady in 2017 (+0.1% the balance of data released from December 2016 to December 2017).

Business confidence, as shown by the Zew index, is growing slightly but remains below the long-term average of 23.7 points. Consumer confidence is growing (data not reported) and in December 2017 has returned to positive after more than ten years.

As for Australia, in the last year, there has been a significant improvement in the labour-market with the unemployment rate dropped by half a percentage point from April to December. Inflation remains slightly below the target while the Retail Sales figure does not yet show a marked recovery in consumption.

The final phase of the analysis concerns the reading of the last Statement and Minutes of the two Central Banks. Let's start with the Eurozone; you find below the most significant steps of the last Statement released by the ECB.

"Regarding non-standard monetary policy measures, we confirm that from January 2018 we intend to continue to make net asset purchases under the asset purchase programme (APP), at a monthly pace of €30 billion, until the end of September 2018, or beyond, if necessary.

The incoming information, including our new staff projections, indicates a strong pace of economic expansion and a significant improvement in the growth outlook. This assessment is broadly reflected in the December 2017 Eurosystem staff macroeconomic projections for the Euro area. These projections foresee annual real GDP increasing by 2.4% in 2017, 2.3% in 2018, 1.9% in 2019 and 1.7% in 2020. Compared with the September 2017 ECB staff macroeconomic projections, the outlook for real GDP growth has been revised up substantially.

Private consumption is underpinned by ongoing employment gains, which are also benefiting from past labour-market reforms, and by rising household wealth

Business investment continues to strengthen on the back of very favourable financing conditions, rising corporate profitability and strengthening demand."

From the last Statement released by the <u>Reserve Bank of Australia</u>:

"The outlook for non-mining business investment has improved further, with the forward-looking indicators being more positive than they have been for some time. Increased public infrastructure investment is also supporting the economy.

Employment growth has been strong over 2017 and the unemployment rate has declined. Employment has been rising in all states and has been accompanied by a rise in labour force participation.

There are reports that some employers are finding it more difficult to hire workers with the necessary skills. However, wage growth remains low, and this means there is uncertainty in the outlook for household consumption. Household incomes are growing slowly, and debt levels are high.

The Australian Dollar remains within the range that it has been in over the past two years. An appreciating exchange rate would be expected to result in a slower pick-up in economic activity and inflation than currently forecast."

Once you have finished your analysis, you can draw the appropriate conclusions.

We can sum up: both economies are registering higher growth than the estimates a year earlier. Data regarding employment (even though we have two very different rates of unemployment) are improving, but consumer spending is running late.

The difference is the end of the ECB's Quantitative Easing which has given, and will give, a strong boost to the Euro. That is why <u>EURAUD is expected to rise in the medium to long-term</u>.

However, the probable devaluation of the US Dollar as a result of Trump's protectionist policy and the increase in the price of gold should bring benefits to the Australian Dollar in the short-term, as in a fall of the currency pair.

In the case of a decline of EURAUD below 1.48000 (the most recent cut in interest rates of the Reserve Bank of Australia), it would create an excellent opportunity to open a long position on the currency pair, but you are still very far away from this. A good strategy is to place a spy-order in the area 1.52000 (sensitive area); As it is in fact very likely that EURAUD will start a new bullish phase from that level.

Before I end of this chapter, I will highlight the four key steps to make a correct analysis of a currency pair, to understand which of the two currencies and therefore economies is the strongest.

1. First step: take the chart and highlight the key levels, both macroeconomic and sensitive levels for the market (at the beginning, you can draw static supports and resistances).

2. Second step: highlight the pros and cons of each of the economies that make up the currency pair.

3. Third step: analyse the two economies through their macroeconomic data. I advise taking data from at least the last 18/24 months for a better breakdown.

4. Fourth step: read the last Statement and Minutes, and underline the most significant steps, just as I did in the analyses you have seen in this chapter.

Now that you understand my process and framework which I have thoroughly explained the correct method in its various phases that the investment banks apply to analyse a currency pair. Be cognisant, it is nothing more than comparing two economies.

To put it succinctly investment bank traders do not use technical analysis, nor do they use indicators on their charts. They do not use trading systems or expert advisors attached on the Metatrader platform.

While a significant part of the entire process of analysis requires experience in the field, and this is an aspect that is difficult to teach. At best, I can give advice dictated by my own experience.

BONDS AND CURRENCIES

CHAPTER 23

～

Corporations, governments, and municipalities utilise a variety of options to raise capital. In addition to issuing bonds in domestic markets and local currencies, governments and companies can also issue bonds in other markets and in different currencies. Since interest rates may differ from country to country, issuers may choose to take advantage of these opportunities.

Bond yields play a major role in determining the direction of a currency. The difference between one country's bond yield and another country's bond yield, known as the interest rate differential, is more influential on the direction of a currency than the actual bond yield.

The interest rate differential between the bond yields of two countries normally moves parallel to the relevant currency pair, more precisely, an increasing interest rate differential helps to strengthen the higher-yielding currency, whilst a decreasing differential acts positively for the lower-yielding currency.

Short-term interest rates are usually driven by central bank policies, while bond yields fluctuate more with market sentiment. Bond prices move in the opposite direction to their yield. For example, when prices go up, yield goes down.

Understanding the inverse relationship between price and yield is crucial. When interest rates rise, the price of a bond falls because its coupons become less attractive to potential buyers and vice versa.

In addition to this, if a bond is paying a higher coupon rate than the current rates available on new issues of similar-quality bonds, it is likely that the market price will increase, because other investors will be willing to pay more to earn higher interest. Conversely, if a bond is paying a lower coupon than is generally available, other investors will expect to pay less and the market price could decline.

Let me unpack the essential concept for those who are not familiar with the bond market. The yield of a bond refers to the rate of return or interest paid to the bondholder, while the price of a bond is the amount of money the bondholder pays for the bond. Bond yields differentials usually move parallel to currency pairs. This phenomenon occurs because capital flows are attracted to higher-yielding currencies.

When the rate of one currency rises relative to another, investors are attracted to the higher-yielding currency. In addition to this, the cost of owning the lower-yielding currency increases as a bond yield differential moves in favour of the currency being sold. For example, the cost of owning Yen and selling US Dollar will increase when US bond yields rise relative to those of Japanese bonds.

Let's see this in practice with a first example. You can see an example in Figure 55 with the 10-year yield spread between the Australian dollar and the US dollar, and the AUDUSD chart.

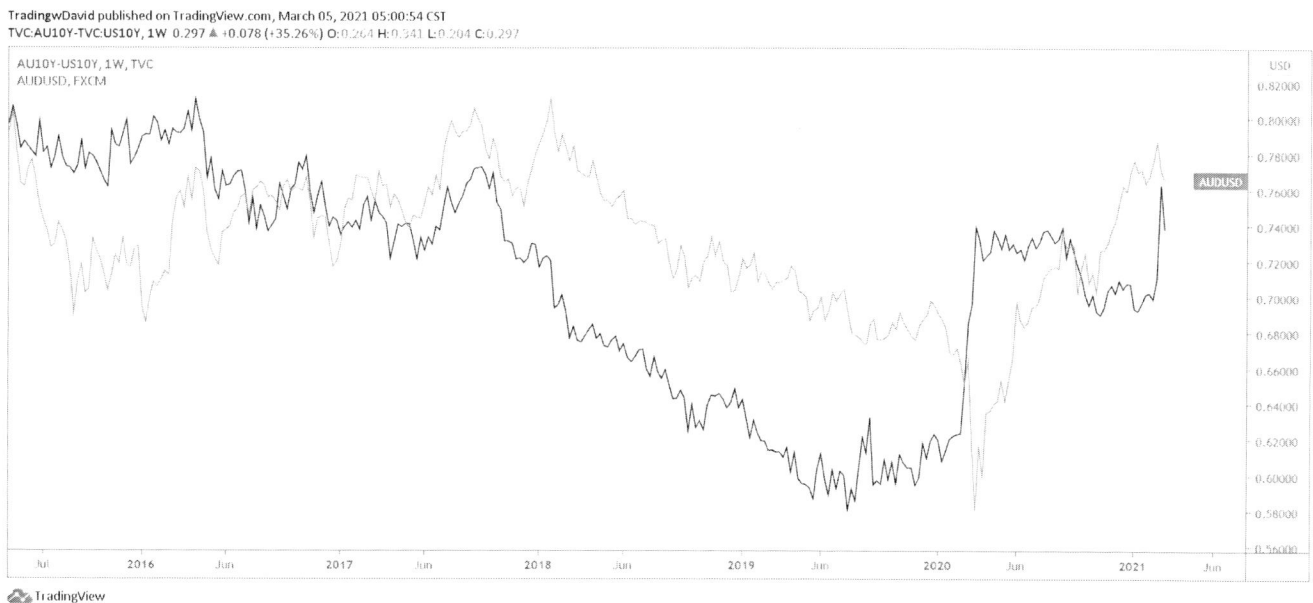

Figure 55 - AU10 Year yield / US10 Year yield, and AUDUSD (TradingView)

Note, most of the time the two lines move parallel to each other. The chart shows that the 10-year yield spread between the Australian dollar and the US dollar (black line) fell between 2018 and 2020. This coincided with a large fall in the Australian dollar against the US dollar (orange line).

When the interest rate differential started to widen again in early 2020, the Australian dollar accentuated its fall because of the Covid-19 crisis, which by this point had begun to hit the markets. Shortly afterwards, however, it aligned itself at the yield differential by rising again and reaching early 2018 levels.

Let's take two more examples. In Figure 56 you can see the 10-year yield spread between the German euro and the US dollar, and the EURUSD chart.

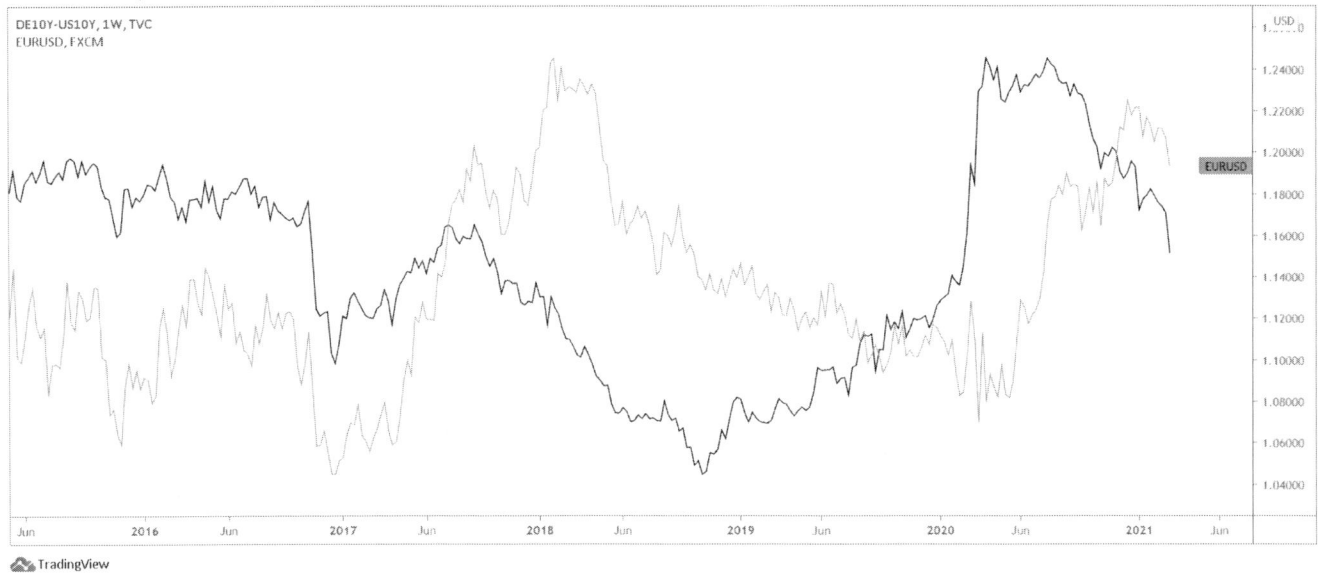

Figure 56 - DE10Year yield / US10 Year yield, and EURUSD (TradingView)

The interest rate differential (black line) peaked in the summer of 2017, while EURUSD (blue line) did not peak until early 2018. Similarly, the interest rate differential hit a low in late 2018, but the EURUSD pair continued to fall until spring 2020.

Again, in Figure 57, you can see the interest rate differential of the 10-year yield spread between the UK pound and the US dollar, and the GBPUSD chart.

Figure 57 - UK10Year yield / US10Year yield, and GBPUSD (TradingView)

Notice how we have confirmation of the movement, almost in unison, of the two lines, with the GBPUSD highs and lows sliding forward by at least six months.

A final example. Below, you can see the chart for AUDCHF together with the AU10Y-CH10Y yield differential (Figure 58).

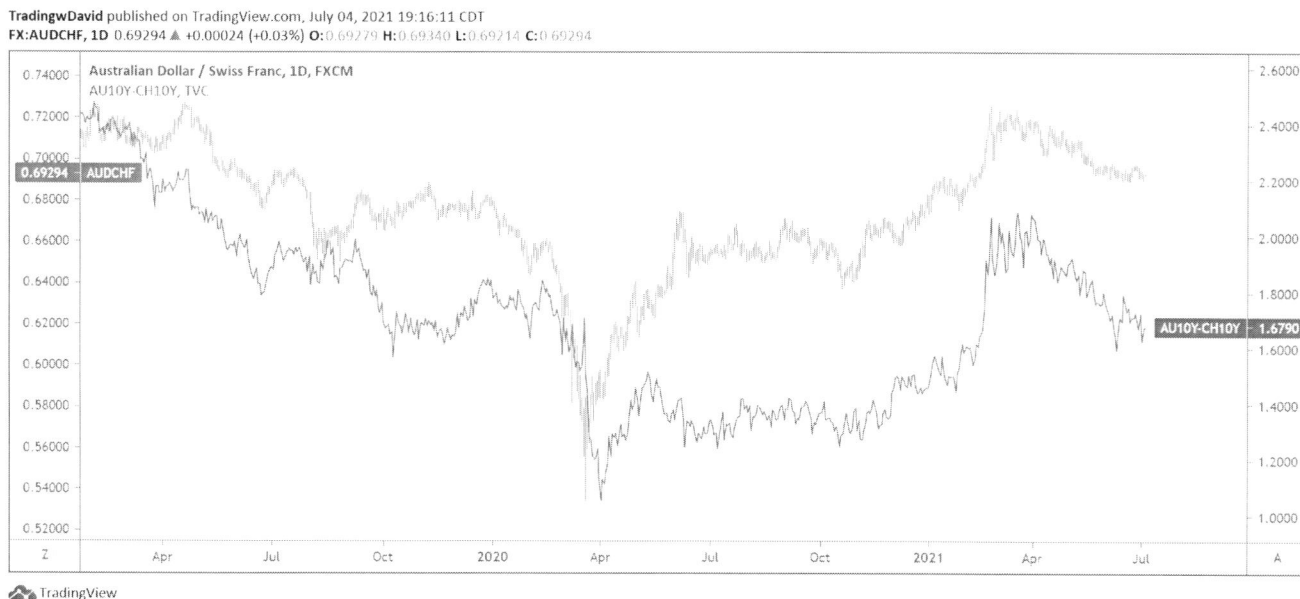

Figure 58 - AU10 Year yield / CH10Year yield, and AUDCHF (TradingView)

We can see how well the two charts correlate. So far, I have shown you that ten (but also five) year bond yield spreads can be used to analyse currencies. The key rule is that when the yield spread widens in favour of a certain currency, that currency will appreciate against the other currencies.

Remember, these relationships favour a long-term strategy. For example, a currency pair could reach a low level a year after the interest rate differential has reached its low. A great deal of patience is therefore required. Do not get caught up in the excitement of the moment.

The important thing in this chapter is the Bond/Yield relationship which gives your analysis new clues or confirmations. If you look back at GBPUSD example – the pair already touched its low in August 2019 and had already aligned with the rate differential then began rising again – and with the arrival of the virus, it was pushed down once more, touching a new low in March 2020. The takeaway here is that you need to evaluate the bigger picture of the information you gained.

INTEREST RATE

CHAPTER 24

~

Interest rates are of great importance in trading, not only in currencies. Sometimes the outcome of a FOMC meeting is known days in advance, but at other times, there is more uncertainty.

Most definitely, there have been times in your trading life when you have wondered what decisions the Federal Reserve would make on interest rates at its next meeting. At the beginning of my career as a trader, I remember that several FOMC meetings, chaired at the time by Alan Greenspan, had uncertain outcomes.

To help market participants, there is a tool available that calculates the probability of the Federal Reserve raising or cutting interest rates, let's look at this tool and delve into it.

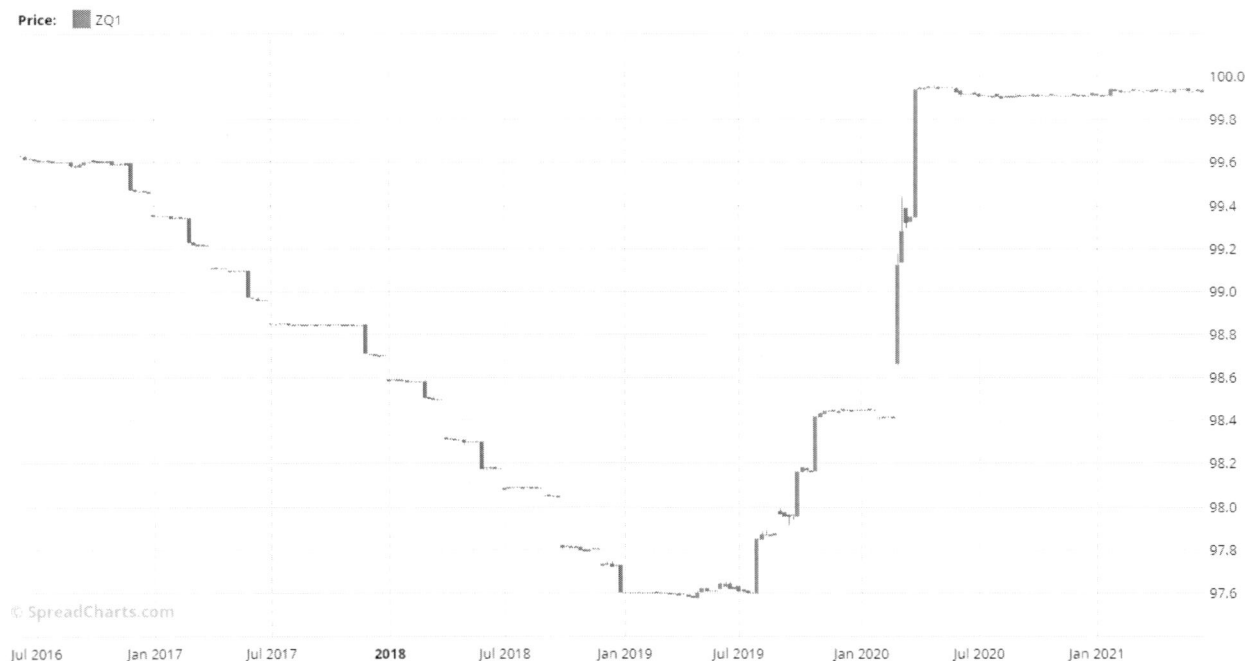

Figure 59 - 30-day Fed Fund Futures (SpreadCharts.com)

The Federal Funds Rate is one of the most influential interest rates in the U.S. To hedge against or express a view on potential changes in short-term interest rates, market participants turn to 30-day Fed Fund Futures contracts (Ticker: ZQ). You can see the chart in Figure 59 above.

30-Day Fed Funds futures is one of the most widely used tools for hedging short-term interest rate risk. Fed Fund futures is a direct reflection of collective marketplace insight regarding the future course of the Federal Reserve's monetary policy.

These contracts are listed monthly and are priced at 100 minus the expected fed funds rate. For example: if the current month's contract is priced at 99, and the market expects the average federal funds effective rate during that month to be 1%, they would thus calculate 100 minus 99.

Using this information, the CME Group created the FedWatch Tool. This tool acts as a barometer for market participants to gauge the markets expectation of potential changes to the fed funds target rate while assessing potential Fed movements around FOMC meetings.

How FedWatch works: first of all, there are some Fed Watch Tool Assumptions and Interpretations:

- The probability of a rate hike is calculated by adding the probabilities of all target rate levels above the current target rate.
- Probabilities of possible Fed Funds target rates are based on Fed Fund futures contract prices, assuming that the rate hike is 0.25% (25 basis points) and that the Fed Funds Effective Rate (FFER) will react by a like amount.
- FOMC meetings probabilities are determined from the corresponding CME Group Fed Fund futures contracts.

The FedWatch tool calculates unconditional probabilities of FOMC meeting outcomes to generate a binary probability tree. The CME Group lists 30-Day Federal Funds Futures, prices of which incorporate market expectations of average daily Federal Funds Effective Rate (FFER) levels during futures contract months. (E.g., the market price for FFK1 reflects the market consensus expectation of the average FFER level during the month of May 2021).

The FFER is published by the Federal Reserve Bank of New York each day and is calculated as a weighted, average transaction-volume of the previous day's rates on trades, arranged by major brokers in the market for overnight unsecured loans between depository institutions.

I will spare you the whole calculation. If you are interested, I refer you to an article on my blog where I quantify the FedWatch calculation (https://tradingwithdavid.com/en/how-to-predict-the-change-in-the-interest-rate/).

I will now show you how to read the FedWatch. The FOMC target range is currently set as 0.00 to 0.25 percent (or 0 to 25 basis points). First, you should select the tool's output for the nearest meeting, which has two potential outcomes, as is displayed in Figure below.

Below in Figure 60, you find the chart from the 17th of May 2021, referring to the FOMC meeting on June 16th, with two bars. The bar on the left represents the probability that rates are unchanged. The bar on the right shows the probability that rates will be increased by a single, 25 basis point-increment, to a target range of 25 to 50 basis points.

MEETING INFORMATION						PROBABILITIES		
MEETING DATE	CONTRACT	EXPIRES	MID PRICE	PRIOR VOLUME	PRIOR OI	EASE	NO CHANGE	HIKE
16 giu 2021	ZQM1	30 giu 2021	99,9325	9.223	105.582	0,0%	94,0%	6,0%

Target Rate Probabilities for 16 giu 2021 Fed Meeting

Current Target Rate of 0-25

TARGET RATE (BPS)	PROBABILITY(%)			
	NOW*	1 DAY 25 MAG 2021	1 WEEK 19 MAG 2021	1 MONTH 26 APR 2021
0-25 (Current)	94,0%	94,0%	90,0%	90,0%
25-50	6,0%	6,0%	10,0%	9,9%
50-75	0,0%	0,0%	0,0%	0,2%

*Data as of 26 mag 2021 04:57:12 CT

Figure 60 - Fed Watch 17th of May 2021 (CME Group)

On May 17th, the probability that interest rates will be raised by 25 basis points at the FOMC meeting on June 16th is 6%. Below the chart, you may also choose to compare the current data with that of one day, one week and one month before.

In the menu on the left there are several interesting entries which I suggest that you explore, to see what information you might get from them. I just want to briefly mention the "chart" entry in the "Dot Plot" section in Figure 61.

Four times per year, the FOMC publishes a dot plot which represents a single FOMC member's assessments of appropriate monetary policy. Each of the 17 dots in each column corresponds to one of the member's expectations for the midpoint of the target range, or a target level, of the federal funds rate.

The CME FedWatch Tool also offers market participants an easy comparison of the FOMC's stated projections against those priced into the futures market. The dots marked in light blue represent the median projection among the members while the dots marked in red represent the effective rate implied by the year-end Fed Fund futures price.

The CME FedWatch Tool can be a valuable instrument for those managing risks or hedging against changes in Fed monetary policy. You can find the tool here: https://www.cmegroup.com/trading/interest-rates/countdown-to-fomc.html.

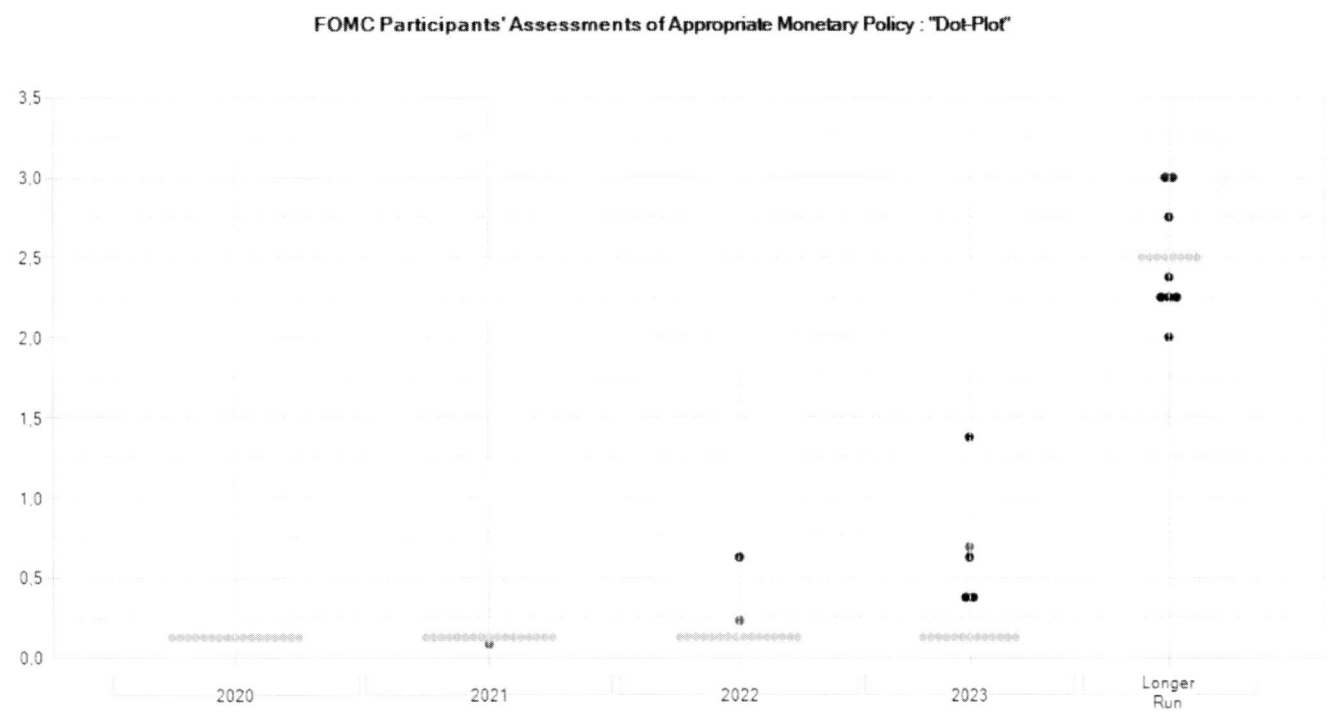

Figure 61 - Fed Watch Dot Plot menu (CME Group)

Now, let me show you how I use the 30-day Fed Funds Futures. I use is a spread built with 30-day Fed Funds futures, namely, the futures of the previous month minus the delivery by which I need to know the probability of an interest rate hike/cut.

Reading such a spread is very simple. For instance, let me take the spread ZQN21-

ZQZ22. The value represents the differential in basis points between the current rate and the rate expected in December 2022.

If the spread is 0.00, the probability that the Fed will raise interest rates by December 2022 is 0%. If it is 0.25, the probability is 100% - and in the intermediate values, the higher the percentile the closer the spread gets to 0.25. If the spread is negative, there is no longer a probability of a rise, but rather of a cut in interest rates.

Here is a practical example. Below, you can see the chart ZQN21-ZQZ22 (Figure 62). On Thursday 1st July 2021, the spread closed at 0.237. The probability of the Fed raising interest rates by 25 basis points by December 2022 was 94.8%. Unemployment data released the following day undermined this certainty and the spread closed the week at 0.208. The probability thus fell to 83.2%, with the dollar also heading in the same direction.

Figure 62 - Spread ZQN21-ZQZ22 (SpreadCharts.com)

A week later, the spread closed at 0.178 with a 71.2% probability of a 25 basis point US rate hike by December 2022.

This is a good way to predict an interest rate hike/cut by the Federal Reserve. It is also useful because the reference currency, in this case the dollar, very often moves in unison with the spread.

CARRY TRADE

CHAPTER 25

~

In this chapter we dig deeper into curry trade which we learnt about in Chapters 20 and 21. The chart below of USDJPY in Figure 63.

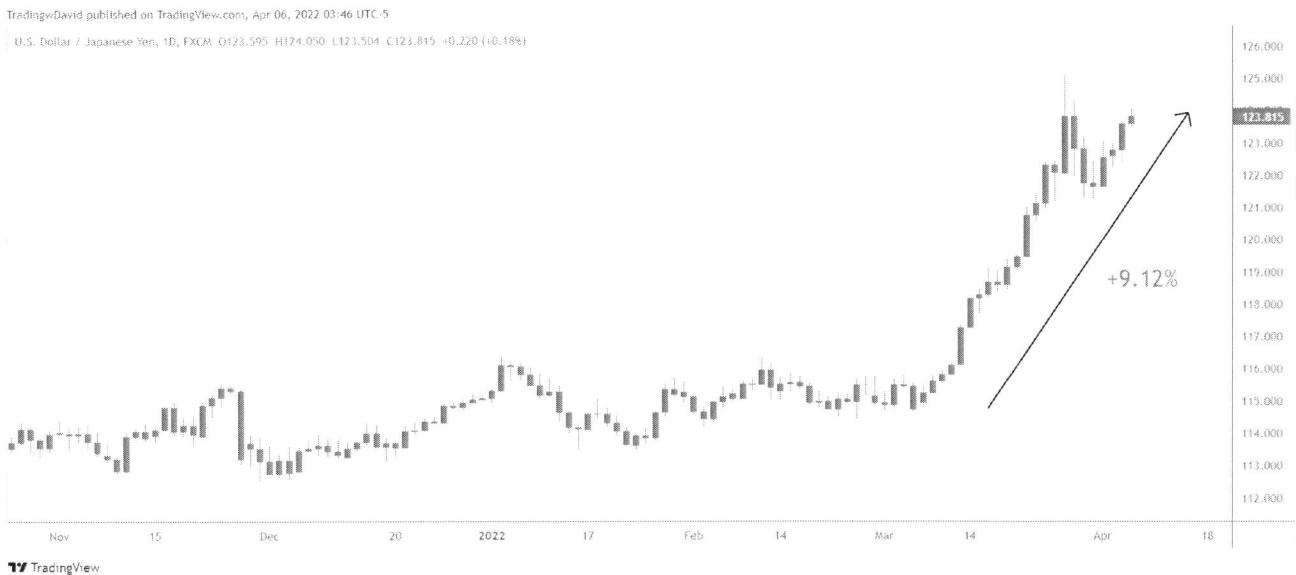

Figure 63 - USDJPY chart (TradingView)

As you can clearly see, there has been a violent bullish movement in the currency pair in recent weeks. What has generated this strong rise? Speculation, or better, a precise way of speculating USDJPY: the carry trade.

The carry trade is a long-term strategy that identifies the difference in value in "carrying" one financial asset to another financial asset, or the same financial asset at some future time.

For those working with commodities, spread trading can be counted as carry trade. An example? The sale of one type of grain, with the proceeds of which to buy a different one, and to retain the difference in value at the end.

In Forex, the strategy is as old as the financial markets, and consists of borrowing money in countries with a low-yielding currency to invest it in financial instruments (rarely in real assets) in countries with a high-yielding currency. The profit obtained is equal to the difference between the return on the investment and the cost of financing.

It is well documented, however, that exchange rate changes do not compensate for interest rate differentials. If anything, the opposite is true empirically: high interest rate currencies tend to appreciate while low interest rate currencies tend to depreciate. Consequently, the carry trade is a profitable investment strategy.

For a carry trade to be profitable, however, it is necessary for the currencies chosen to benefit from an exchange rate that is almost stable over time and especially between the time the loan is taken out and the time it is repaid. If this is not the case, exchange rate losses will reduce the realised gains, with the risk that the investment will produce a loss. The investment is usually in low-risk instruments, such as government bonds.

I leave aside all theoretical discourse, which are as interesting as they are unhelpful for the purpose and concentrate only on the practical part. I therefore return to the example above. On the one hand, there is the Yen, the currency always preferred for this type of operation. With interest rates in negative territory since 2016, the Japanese yen is once again emerging as an appropriate funding currency. On the other hand, the United States with the seven rate increases planned for 2022. A mix that prompted institutional investors to buy USDJPY, pushing it up 9.12% in little more than three weeks.

USDJPY is not the only currency pair used to make the carry trade, there are others that lend themselves well to this strategy. For example, another widely used carry trade technique is to borrow Swiss Francs and then use them to buy European currencies (excluding Euro).

Due to the zero-interest rate policy adopted by the ECB to support consumption within Europe, and to decrease the interest cost pressure on the balance of the most indebted European countries, the Euro has entered the group of currencies to be borrowed.

The narrative is that investments are made mainly with capital borrowed in Yen, Swiss Franc and in recent years in Euro, and have been used mainly to buy bonds in US Dollars, commodity currencies (Australian and New Zealand Dollars) and from 2022, also in British Pounds. Emerging market bonds are riskier, although more profitable.

It will not have escaped that the two most commonly used funding currencies are JPY and CHF, the refuge currencies par excellence. The carry trade is only used when markets are risk-on, that is, investors have a high appetite for risk, and so, they sell Yen and Swiss Francs to buy US, Australian and New Zealand Dollars.

However, extraordinary events occur that affect financial markets differently.

One of the most, if not the most, used currency pairs in the carry trade is AUDJPY. We have seen this chart already with the currency pair and the VIX Index (Figure 64).

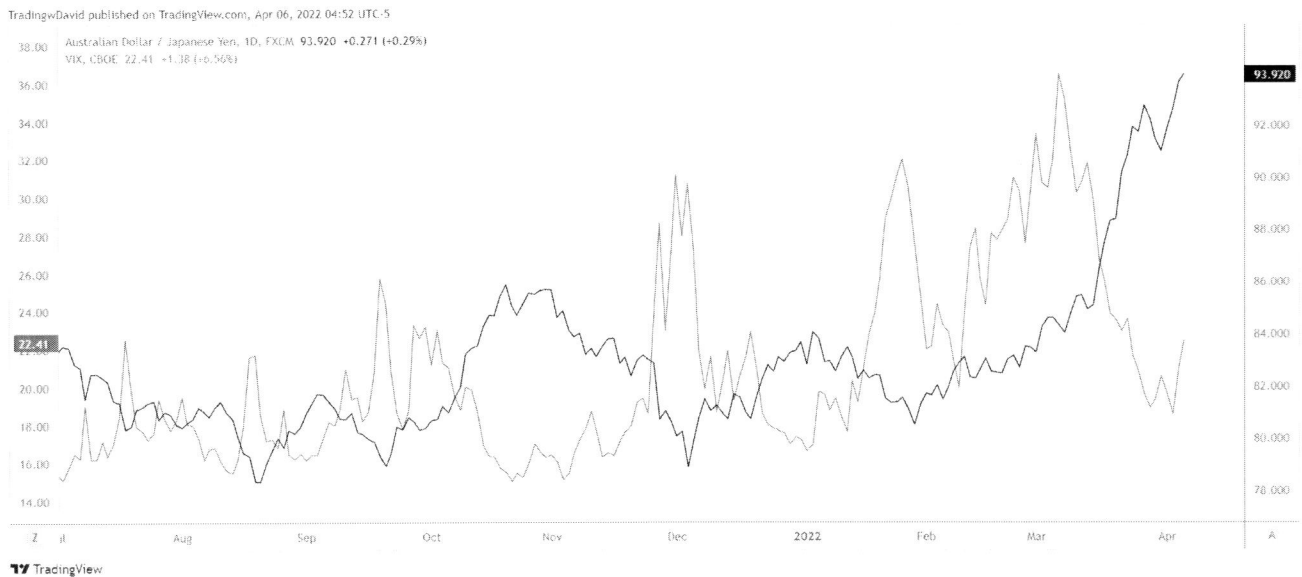

Figure 64 - AUDUSD and VIX Index (TradingView)

AUDJPY and VIX Index are inversely correlated, as one rises, the other falls, and vice versa. Remember in Chapter 20, in February 2022, both the currency pair and the VIX Index had a bullish movement. The reason for this was the sharp rise in commodity prices following the outbreak of war in Ukraine which benefited the commodity currencies, with AUD and NZD appreciating against all other currencies.

When trading currencies, you certainly must understand the macro narrative and the current environment of the monetary policy of central banks, read the statements and speeches of chairmen and evaluate economies through key macroeconomic data and any future actions mean, also do not ignore the effect of carry trade on certain currency pairs, exogenous events and anything else that can affect Forex.

With this strategy, you need to pay close attention to the costs. In Forex all positions are technically closed by the broker at the end of each day, even though the market is open 24 hours a day, 5 days a week. The broker will close and reopen your position and then credit or debit you with the difference in the overnight interest rate of the currency you sold and the currency you bought – this is known as "swap" and is used to inform traders of the real debit or credit of the interest rate differential. Many brokers if not all add their own costs. More often than you think, you may have to pay interest to the broker whether you buy or sell the same currency pair.

Before you make a carry trade – and to avoid any nasty surprises, take a look at the swap rate charged by your broker. Although, personally, I do not know any traders who use the carry trade strategy. But even so, do not disregard it as institutional investors use it, so keep it in mind when analysing specific currency pairs.

DIVERSIFICATION OF PORTFOLIO

CHAPTER 26

My first years in Forex were a disaster. I was great at losing money. I had studied all sorts of indicators and oscillators. I had studied computers at university, so I had created Expert Advisors (automated strategies "attached" to Metatrader platform) increasingly complex because they worked for me while I was enjoying the money earned in some Caribbean paradise.

Nothing could be more wrong; I neglected a very important fact: markets are in constant state of evolution. They do not always move in the same way. There will be more volatile periods and others less so, periods of trend and others in congestion.

An example that I often make is comparing markets activity to going all-year round in the same clothes. Seasons change just like markets do, and it is not possible (or at least wise) to go dressed in the same way throughout the year, just like you cannot use a strategy profitably in every situation of the market.

With this I am not saying that automated trading is a waste of money. No, but it is not suitable for a single strategy. I do not know how many of you know Andrea Unger, he was 4 times world champion in trading. He does automated trading with the "Unger method". Basically, he has over 200 strategies applied to a currency pair.

What does it mean to always operate with the same strategy? A strategy may have been good for years, but within these years it will have favourable moments, and others less so. Working with a single strategy means having great experience and knowing when to use it and when not to. It means being very disciplined and being prepared to withstand possible negative situations, even for a long period of time.

Managing a portfolio means covering yourself, learning to develop more strategies on the market so that you can ensure you overcome any and every situation – since one strategy can be causing trouble whilst another giving a profit, it is essential, therefore, to have equilibrium in your portfolio (just like Andrea Unger did with his method).

For example, you may be in trend, and you can exploit it with the spot Forex by buying or selling a currency pair. If the market moves sideways, instead, you can be nondirectional using the options on the currency futures.

You saw another example of this in one of the previous chapters, with the safe-haven currencies. You can balance your portfolio using CHF or JPY to cover some more aggressive trade.

These and other measures, all put together, create a portfolio. The portfolio tends to protect you in times of trouble by using the proper balancing. This concept is the basis of how to manage your money and how to invest your savings. I have not yet found the perfect strategy that works for every occasion, but I suspect that it does not exist.

In this way, you get more cards to play, you compensate those times when a strategy loses a bit of effectiveness or has fewer opportunities. In that case, you can use another strategy, so you have a diversification of portfolio always effective, and when you are losing on the one hand, you are gaining from another. That is, in my opinion, the perfect structure to get you comfortable in every market situation.

I will end this short chapter by explaining how I divided my Forex portfolio, just to give you an idea of how I work. It is divided into three parts:

- 10% for intraday operations. It is rare, but occasionally I also make "hit-and-run" trades, particularly during NFP (Non-Farm Payrolls)
- 75% for medium-term operations following the fundamental analysis of the currencies
- 15% in liquidity

Withdrawals: (of total assets). I withdraw monthly 100% of profits obtained from intraday operations, at least 50% of those obtained with the medium-term activity, and I leave on the account the gains got in the long-term savings plan (that does not involve Forex).

Every two or three months, I make a rebalancing of the whole portfolio with percentages that remain unchanged.

MONEY MANAGEMENT

CHAPTER 27

∽

Money management is the mainstay and the cornerstone of your investments, and most important skill in trading. Few traders adopt proper money management, for this reason, approximately 85% of traders lose all their money in a few months.

The money management system consists of position size, it refers to the number of units of capital to be invested in each trade and the allocation of money on the various assets in the portfolio, and risk management, which analyse the risk linked to the position taken in the market. You can find more information about this in my book: "*Behavioural Finance - Psychology and Money Management.*"

A successful trader who gets steady profits over time follows the rules of money management in an absolute rigid way. From the very beginning of your trading business, you must determine the percentage of your equity to allocate to each trade. Your first thought should be directed to the protection and preservation of the money but only after its maximisation.

One of the adages of Wall Street says: "*cut the losses short and let the profits run.*" summarises the concept perfectly, as it implies to keep losses small if it deviates from your plan and only then encourages to let profits runs if it goes according to your trade playbook.

Money protection must be your absolute priority because being a trader includes taking losses. Anyone who tells you that he has never incurred losses from trading, is either lying or never traded. In order to survive in the long run, you want to analyse the market correctly before you open a trade, determine every aspect of risk management and be confident with the plan you put together. This way you will know how much you can lose and will not find yourself in trouble when you face a drawdown. The more you are aware of how much you could lose, the more stress-free and tranquil the trade will be.

Trading is an entrepreneurial profession, something that has to give you an income, but at the same time must not be a burden or worsen your quality of life. The most important aspect of trading is risk control. To achieve this, I emphasise, you need to have a well-defined trading process which you will always stick to and respect.

Money management is something personal, nobody can tell you how you should manage your trades. We are all different people and have different traits, emotions, expectations, risk appetite etc. So, you must build your own trading scenarios based on yourself, not on what others decide. Now, I am going to explain how I work, how I manage my trades just as an example, so you can get an idea of how to structure your money management.

As I mentioned earlier, I like to set up a wide-ranging operation by which even when there is a movement against my position, it will not put a strain on my overall trade plan, and I can manage the operation with confidence. I start with my first order for testing the market, a "spy order" usually of a small amount at most 1/3 of the entire order, of course, always proportionate to the equity. Then, I add a higher "primary order", relative to the size, just to rebalance the average price and be able to manage the operation better.

Now, what should be the dimensions of the spy order and primary order? When I decide to open a spy order, I determine the size according to the maximum loss of the entire operation. For example, I choose to risk for every medium-term Forex trade at most 1.50% of my equity. 1.50% is divided into 0.75% for the spy order and 0.75% of the primary order which is opened closer to the stop-loss than the spy order and which will have greater size. This is just an example; you can decide different percentages based on your risk appetite.

Figure 65 - AUDUSD daily chart (TradingView.com)

Money Management is a detrimental part of the strategy. If for example, I buy a currency pair too soon, I risk getting an average price that can cause an issue later. Being greedy in trading can be disastrous if you don't understand the principles of risk assessment. Let me give an example to understand how better to choose the size of the two orders. Let's look at AUDUSD chart again, for convenience, you see above in Figure 65 above.

Once I have completed my detailed analysis from every angle, I decided to sell AUDUSD. So, I put a spy order at 0.80400 and a primary order at 0.83000 with the stop loss at 0.85000 for both the orders. For the medium-term capital allocation is $30,000 (as an example)

By using the same percentage of loss of the previous example, 0.75% of $ 30,000 is equal to $ 225.00. That means that the maximum loss for the spy order will be $ 225.00, and the maximum loss of the primary order will always be $ 225.00.

At this point, knowing the value of 1 pip ($ 0.10 for each $ 1,000 of investment for AUDUSD), I can calculate the size of the two orders with a simple formula:

[1,000 * (equity * %of max loss) / pips of stop] / value of 1 pip

And for AUDUSD: I calculate the size of the two orders:

Size spy-order = [€ 1,000 * (€ 30,000 * 0.75%) / 460] / € 0.09 = € 5,500

Size primary-order = [€ 1,000 * (€ 30,000 * 0.75%) / 200] / € 0.09 = € 12.500

Hence, I sell AUDUSD with € 5,500 at 0.80400 for the spy order, and I put an order to sell € 12,500 at 0.83000 the primary order. The stop loss is at 0.85000 while I identify the first target in the 0.76000 area. The target must not be too ambitious and must also be in the sensitive areas of the currency pair by using subjective probability or Volume Profile. This is basically my way of managing a trade.

One consideration, the stop-loss level is fixed, and stays at that level, you have to close the trade with no excuses, even if you don't reach the target – you also need to monitor the movement and observe how quickly the currency pair reaches the chosen level and the speed at which it moves a currency pair. If, for example, you get a profit 200/250 pips in 2-3 days, you can consider splitting the trade, by taking a partial profit or closing at least a part of it.

When a movement is swift, you must always evaluate the trade and not be greedy, because as I have said, the difference between being greedy and letting the profit run is very subtle. At this point, you must be wondering: how do I calculate the pip value of a currency pair? you will find that, in Appendix A where you have the answer.

VALUE–AT–RISK

CHAPTER 28

~

Value-at-Risk (VaR) measures the potential loss in value of a risky asset or portfolio over a defined period for a given confidence interval. Thus, if the VaR on EURUSD is 1.81% at one-week, 95% confidence level, there is an only 5% chance that the value of EURUSD will drop more than 1.81% over any given week.

Value at Risk is used by commercial and investment banks to capture the potential loss in value of their traded portfolios from adverse market movements over a specified period, this can then be compared to their available capital and cash reserves to ensure that the losses can be covered without putting the firms at risk. But you can use VaR in a different way to decide where to set the stop loss.

How? For example, if you decide to buy EURUSD (current price 1.0554), if you put a stop-loss 1.81% away from your entry price (that is, 1.0363), theoretically, you will have 95% probability of not seeing it met by the price. It is the best way to decide the stop loss logic, it removes any doubts you might have and all the emotions. But before I explain the calculation, let's take a look at some aspects of VaR and its main three key elements:

1. a specified level of loss in value
2. a fixed time period over which risk is assessed (1 day, 1 week, etc.)
3. a confidence interval (usually 95% or 99%)

The VaR can be specified for an individual asset, a portfolio of assets or an entire firm, and the idea behind it is volatility. Three basic approaches are used to compute Value-at-Risk, though there are numerous variations within each approach.

- <u>Historical method</u>. It represents the simplest way of estimating the Value at Risk for many assets and portfolios. In this approach, the VaR for a portfolio is estimated by creating a hypothetical time series of returns on that portfolio, obtained by running the portfolio through actual historical data and computing the changes that would have occurred in each period.

- Variance-Covariance method. It assumes that the daily price returns for a given position follow a normal distribution. From the distribution of daily returns calculated from daily price series, you estimate the standard deviation. The daily Value-at-Risk (VaR) is simply a function of the standard deviation and the desired confidence level.

- Monte Carlo simulation. The approach is similar to the Historical method except for one big difference. The hypothetical data set used is generated by a statistical distribution rather than historical price levels. The assumption is that the selected distribution captures or reasonably approximates price behaviour of the assets or portfolios.

Which one to use? The most robust results are likely to come from the historical method. This is because the approach is not hampered by the normal distribution assumption.

The Variance-Covariance method is the most popular approach. However, it is also the one that receives the most criticism given the normality assumption. The Monte Carlo simulation appears to be fairly attractive, but in most simulators, the default distribution used is also normal. This essentially puts the results in the same category and range as the Variance-Covariance method.

All methods have a common base but then diverge in how they actually calculate Value-at-Risk. They also have a common problem in assuming that the future will follow the past. This shortcoming is normally addressed by supplementing any Value-at-Risk figures with appropriate sensitivity analysis and/or stress testing.

EUR/USD 1.0554 +0.0031 (+0.29%)

General   Chart   News & Analysis   Technical   Forum

Overview | Forward Rates | Historical Data | Related Instruments | Options | Currency Converter | Contracts

EUR/USD Overview   i

| | | 1 5 15 30 1H 5H 1D 1W 1M | | Technical Chart » |

EUR/USD - Euro US Dollar ◆ **1.0554** +0.0031 (+0.29%)

1.0570

1.0560

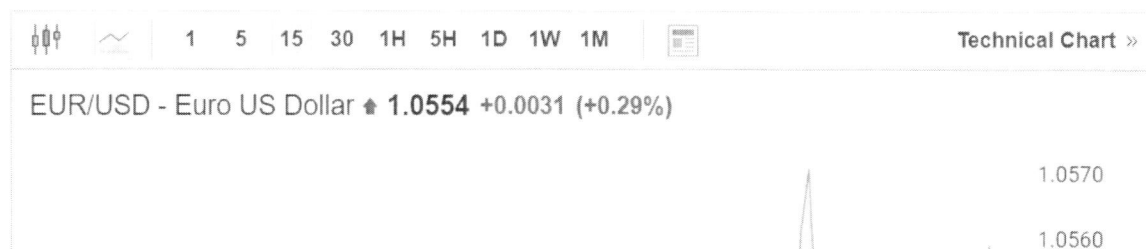

Figure 66 - EURUSD (Investing.com)

Now, let's see the calculation for the Value-at-Risk. In order not to complicate the argument too much, I will use the historical method. You need to go on the investing.com website and search for the currency pair of your interest. In this example, I use EURUSD (Figure 66 above).

Here, you have to click on <u>Historical Data</u> (Figure 67).

EUR/USD Historical Data

Time Frame:

Daily ▼						
Daily			Download Data	26/05/2022 - 26/06/2022 🗓		
Weekly						
Monthly	Price ⁝	Open ⁝	High ⁝	Low ⁝		Change % ⁝
Jun 24, 2022	1.0554	1.0526	1.0572	1.0511		0.29%
Jun 23, 2022	1.0523	1.0567	1.0582	1.0482		-0.40%
Jun 22, 2022	1.0565	1.0527	1.0606	1.0468		0.38%
Jun 21, 2022	1.0525	1.0510	1.0583	1.0508		0.15%
Jun 20, 2022	1.0509	1.0472	1.0546	1.0472		0.10%
Jun 17, 2022	1.0498	1.0548	1.0560	1.0445		-0.46%

Figure 67 - EURUSD Historical Data (Investing.com)

	A	B
1	Date	Close
2		
3	Jun 19, 2022	1,05540
4	Jun 12, 2022	1,04980
5	Jun 05, 2022	1,05150
6	May 29, 2022	1,07180
7	May 22, 2022	1,07270
8	May 15, 2022	1,05600
9	May 08, 2022	1,04110
10	May 01, 2022	1,05510
11	Apr 24, 2022	1,05410
12	Apr 17, 2022	1,07940
13	Apr 10, 2022	1,08060
14	Apr 03, 2022	1,08760
15	Mar 27, 2022	1,10530
16	Mar 20, 2022	1,09810
17	Mar 13, 2022	1,10550
18	Mar 06, 2022	1,09090
19	Feb 27, 2022	1,09260

Figure 68 - EURUSD weekly Close

On the next page, on the left top corner select the <u>Time Frame</u>, <u>Weekly</u>, and then on the top right corner select the date (which has to be at least the last five years). Then, you click on Download Data.

Now, open the file .csv with Excel. The only data you need is the <u>Close</u>, so you can delete everything else, as I did in Figure 68 above.

First, you need to calculate the absolute value of the <u>Return</u> of each week. The formula is simple: you subtract from each close the one immediately below and divide the result by the second of the two values. For the above table, the formula for the first Return is as follows:

=ABS((B3-B4)/B4)

Once you have the first Return value in the first cell - you simply copy and paste the formula on all the other cells, as in Figure 69.

Second, you need to arrange the Return column in descending order. But doing this is not possible since the column is made up of numbers that are the result of a previous calculation. Therefore, you copy the Return column C (Fig.69) and right-click to paste in the next column under Paste Special to choose Values. In cell D the copied Return must be put in a Descending order as in Fig. 70.

	A	B	C
1	Date	Close	Return
2			
3	Jun 19, 2022	1,05540	0,005334349
4	Jun 12, 2022	1,04980	0,001616738
5	Jun 05, 2022	1,05150	0,018940101
6	May 29, 2022	1,07180	0,000839004
7	May 22, 2022	1,07270	0,015814394
8	May 15, 2022	1,05600	0,014311786
9	May 08, 2022	1,04110	0,013268884
10	May 01, 2022	1,05510	0,000948677
11	Apr 24, 2022	1,05410	0,023438948
12	Apr 17, 2022	1,07940	0,001110494
13	Apr 10, 2022	1,08060	0,00643619
14	Apr 03, 2022	1,08760	0,016013752
15	Mar 27, 2022	1,10530	0,00655678
16	Mar 20, 2022	1,09810	0,006693804
17	Mar 13, 2022	1,10550	0,013383445
18	Mar 06, 2022	1,09090	0,001555922
19	Feb 27, 2022	1,09260	0,030265377

Figure 69 - EURUSD weekly Return

	A	B	C	D	E
1	Date	Close	Return	Return Descend.	No.
2					
3	Jun 19, 2022	1,05540	0,005334349	0,041795231	1
4	Jun 12, 2022	1,04980	0,001616738	0,037007023	2
5	Jun 05, 2022	1,05150	0,018940101	0,030265377	3
6	May 29, 2022	1,07180	0,000839004	0,029886914	4
7	May 22, 2022	1,07270	0,015814394	0,027191959	5
8	May 15, 2022	1,05600	0,014311786	0,023487803	6
9	May 08, 2022	1,04110	0,013268884	0,023438948	7
10	May 01, 2022	1,05510	0,000948677	0,020320502	8
11	Apr 24, 2022	1,05410	0,023438948	0,019950998	9
12	Apr 17, 2022	1,07940	0,001110494	0,019318279	10
13	Apr 10, 2022	1,08060	0,00643619	0,018940101	11
14	Apr 03, 2022	1,08760	0,016013752	0,018215375	12
15	Mar 27, 2022	1,10530	0,00655678	0,018070079	13
16	Mar 20, 2022	1,09810	0,006693804	0,017876718	14
17	Mar 13, 2022	1,10550	0,013383445	0,017487539	15
18	Mar 06, 2022	1,09090	0,001555922	0,017372134	16
19	Feb 27, 2022	1,09260	0,030265377	0,016915163	17

Figure 70 - EURUSD Return Descending and Position

Furthermore, you create another column (E) the Return Descending (1, 2, 3, 4, etc.) up to the penultimate value (the last is "#DIV/0!" so not valid). You can see the result of the two operations described above in Figure 70.

At this point, you have all the data to calculate the Value-at-Risk. You leave an empty column (F) to allow for some space. At the top, you put the total data number, which is the last number in the No. column E (Figure 71).

257	Aug 06, 2017	1,18210	0,004162419	0,000178285	255
258	Jul 30, 2017	1,17720	0,001701838	0,000176788	256
259	Jul 23, 2017	1,17520	0,00763097	0,000175932	257
260	Jul 16, 2017	1,16630	0,016915163	0,000086133	258
261	Jul 09, 2017	1,14690	0,005964389	0,000082522	259
262	Jul 02, 2017	1,14010	#DIV/0!	#DIV/0!	

Figure 71 - EURUSD last position number

Now you calculate the VaR (95%). First, you need to use the following formula to find the VaR (95%) position:

$$= (1-95\%)*G3$$

Where G3 is the cell number where I have put the total data number (you will use the cell you have chosen). Below the result in Figure 72.

The VaR (95%) on EURUSD at one-week is the figure on the left of the number 13 of the <u>Return Descending</u> column, that is, 0.018070079, which is 1.81%.

D Return Descend.	E No.	F	G	H	I
0,041795231	1		259		
0,037007023	2				
0,030265377	3		VaR(95%)		13
0,029886914	4				
0,027191959	5				
0,023487803	6				
0,023438948	7				
0,020320502	8				
0,019950998	9				
0,019318279	10				
0,018940101	11				
0,018215375	12				
0,018070079	13				
0,017876718	14				
0,017487539	15				
0,017372134	16				
0,016915163	17				

Figure 72 - EURUSD VaR(95%)

To finish, I add that besides the Var, there is the CVar. Conditional Value-at-Risk (CVaR) is the extended risk measure of Value-at-Risk that quantifies the average loss over a specified time frame of unlikely scenarios beyond the confidence level.

For example, a one-week CVaR(95%) of EURUSD is 2.52% means that the expected loss of the worst 5% scenarios over one week is 2.52%. Conditional Value-at-Risk is also known as Expected Shortfall.

VaR gives you a range of potential losses, whilst CVaR gives you an average of the potential loss. CVaR is generally considered a better approximation of potential losses.

The calculation is very easy. You divide 1 by the number of the position you have found with the VaR calculation (in the example above "13") and then multiply the result by the sum of the first 13 returns (always relative to the example) of the <u>Return Descending</u> column.

The formula for the excel sheet seen above is as follows:

$$=(1/I5)*SUM(D3:D15)$$

The results are in Figure 73.

D	E	F	G	H	I
Return Descend.	No.				
0,041795231	1		259		
0,037007023	2				
0,030265377	3		VaR(95%)	1,81%	13
0,029886914	4		CVaR(95%)	2,52%	
0,027191959	5				
0,023487803	6				
0,023438948	7				

Figure 73 - EURUSD, VaR and CVaR

You have seen the best way to place a stop loss. By using the VaR or the CVar (at your discretion, personally, I use the CVaR), you will not only have found a level that has only a 5% probability of not seeing it met by the price, but you will have eliminated any type of doubt and emotion because you know you worked like an investment bank or fund.

In my view, that percentage should correspond to the maximum loss that you have decided in your trading plan.

SOME COMMENTS PART 2

CHAPTER 29

~

When you trade, unpredictability is a factor you need to consider. Even when you open a trade that seems most certain in all its dynamics, there is always 1-2% of your decision-making that you cannot control. You can consider every detail, and gather all the information, but there is always a percentage that you cannot control. And it is the case for every investment. If you do not start from this premise, you cannot understand trading business.

Central banks are like CEOs of a company, and all of them believe that their company is the best. If in your analyses and considerations something unforeseen happens that changes the outcome, nothing can be done about it. You simply have to accept the change and remember that the stop loss will limit your loss. In any case, by remaining faithful to the established plan, you have nonetheless done a proper analysis.

I have mentioned correlations previously, and you know, that I find them irrelevant with other currencies in Forex, especially in the medium to long-term. Because doing so, you create a relationship between two economies and a third economy. But if this third economy's dynamic changes, your entire analysis becomes obsolete, essentially invalid.

Correlations between currencies are an instrument that is convenient for you when everything goes well, but it causes problems the minute events deviate from the initial course. You obviously cannot know this in hindsight, but those are the moments in which you could really trigger financial ruin to your portfolio and blow your account.

For this reason, I do not recommend that you trade currencies in that manner. You already have a lot to analyse when you divide a currency pair in the two economies concept – you have plethora to work with. Let's not go down the rabbit hole by adding other currencies, because that would simply expand the problem.

When there is no clear context, it is better to take the opportunity of working with greater calm and clarity and wait to see how the situation evolves, rather than jumping in and being immediately directional. For example, working with Options, you can manage your investment and intervene to correct the outcome in case of wrong analysis. You can learn more about options in my book "*Options Relaxing Trading – A Complete Guide for Beginners.*"

Be mindful that you are an investor, you are not a person who buys or sells at random. You have a portfolio that must be maintained balanced and well built. Always prepare diligently and have conviction in your trade idea before investing.

Here are some tips to keep you on the right track, you need to stay far from what you cannot control (high volatility, emotionality). You are better off leaving volatile and dangerous currencies alone, and instead focus your energy on the markets that present the most interesting features to you. From my point of view, working with a currency pair that is too volatile is synonymous with handling a portfolio incorrectly. You run the risk of unbalancing it.

You must also be able to select the best opportunities for your trading style. For example, USA holiday = low liquidity, this is a problem because to move a market that is less liquid is much easier for those who want to speculate with that market.

When there is uncertainty, you should stand firm and not invest. Why should you risk your money in something that you are not sure of? Better to wait for better times. When unexpected scenarios happened that you have not factored in trading plan, it is better to get out and stay out, it is better to run away immediately because these are, statistically, the situations where the most money is lost. You should put yourself in the best condition to work and have odds of success on your side.

I tell you this from experience, you should never chase the price, you must stay focused on your goal. When you have the odds on your side, you use them, but one should never run after the price, otherwise, you risk entering the market hastily, hitting the stop loss, only to see the currency pair go in your direction. I enter the market only at the price I see fit – I give nothing because nothing is given to me by the market. And you should do the same.

The market is made up of expectations. A good example is when central bank is expected to cut interest rates. If this happens, this event has already been priced into the market, and the movement will be minimal. However, if the expectation fails, the movement that will follow it will be very strong because we experienced disappointment due to unfulfilled expectations.

At the start of the book, I discussed the importance of getting to know the currencies and their pairs, whilst acquiring experience. I can confirm this from experience traders who master one area succeed much more often than traders that dabble in every market. Let's look at, GBPUSD trait – the pair is very volatile and with any important news it will be strongly speculated. It is among the most speculated currency pairs because within it, it has two of the most traded currencies, particularly the Pound Sterling is very volatile. Whereas the

EURUSD pair is the two most liquid currencies, however, it is the GBPUSD that creates the largest movement, as a percentage, among the majors, it is not a currency pair that you trade directionally with ease – but it becomes advantageous to trade it with Options to capitalise on the volatility.

A similar outcome with the NZD. To trade you need to pair it with a stronger currency such as USD. When you contrast a weaker currency such as NZD (New Zealand Dollar) with a stronger currency like the USD, the speed at which the currency pair will move in the direction of the stronger currency is amplified, much more than the opposite. This concept is fundamental, especially when you use Options.

The difficulty of a trader is to note and see the changes in scenarios on which you have based your strategy. Many times, ego and stubbornness are what makes resist and the voice inside your head says, no, this trade must go well, and when it doesn't you bang your head against the wall and find yourself in the hole with significant losses. Successful traders combine a verity of skills and awareness they are always ready to modify their analysis when the scenario changes.

Sometimes, even the positions closed in profit could have been better managed. You should be self-critical reviewing everything and assess whether you have done your job correctly or if there are points where you made mistakes. For this reason, it is essential to keep a trading journal.

Remember that in trading, the simplest things are always the best, and the ones that last the longest.

ODDS ON YOUR SIDE

CHAPTER 30

~

A phrase I often repeat, whatever market you trade, you should never forget the importance of having the odds of success on your side. In this short chapter, I will show how to conduct a proper analysis by having the odds of success on your side, thus you will close most of the trades in profit. Here are three brief analyses I have written both on my website and TradingView account. I start with EURCHF (analysis made on April 24, 2019) followed by AUDUSD.

Figure 74 - EURCHF daily chart (TradingView.com)

"In the last weeks, CHF (Swiss Franc) has been very weak against all the major currencies. Most likely there is more than one reason for it, including the SNB (Swiss National Bank) that has sold Swiss Francs and bought Euros (as it has often done in the last four and a half years).

I chose EURCHF because it has reached an interesting level. Above you can see the daily chart (Figure 74). Two aspects are shown in the chart. First, the price has reached an important area of resistance (1.14700/1.15000) that will hardly break easily. And second, the 1.13600 level (approximately), the price of EURCHF on March 7, the day Draghi announced a new TLTRO for September during the ECB meeting.

The TLTRO (Targeted Longer-Term Refinancing Operations) which is the loan of money by the ECB to the credit sector (banks) at particularly favourable conditions, lasting four years to alleviate the problems of collection of European banks and support loans to families and businesses. In other words, different names (Quantitative Easing and TLTRO) but the same type of operation (loans non-repayable to banks). Yes, because I strongly doubt that at the end of the four years, the banks will repay the loan.

All this translates into greater liquidity in the markets and, therefore, depreciation of the Euro. And if in the short-term it is the speculation that moves a currency pair, in the medium to long-term it is the fundamentals that decide the right exchange rate. For this reason, in the coming weeks, you will see a return of EURCHF, as the first target, in the 1.12000 area.

There would be the possibility of making a speech about CHF as a safe-haven currency in times of crisis but given the trend of Wall Street and the new highs reached (Nasdaq) or about to be reached (S&P 500), it would still be a premature speech. However, selling EURCHF to cover the upward investment in equities and balancing the portfolio could be a wise idea."

Figure 75 - EURCHF daily chart (TradingView.com)

In this case, the TLTRO was a strong signal of a future weakening of the Euro. Furthermore, the macroeconomic resistance that formed with the announcement was just below an area of resistance, which was broken in the past, only after the announcement by Draghi of the end of Quantitative Easing.

In addition, if EURCHF were to be used as a cover for other operations, including equities (and Wall Street was headed towards a new absolute high at that period), the odds of success in the trade were definitely on my side. Above, you can see the same chart about three months later (Figure 75).

In the following weeks, EURCHF started a bearish trend, going even beyond the second target of my trade to 1,10000.

You can read the analysis on TradingView https://www.tradingview.com/chart/EURCHF/wa3ZxMi8-Eur-Chf-Analysis.

Now, let's see the next example, AUDUSD (analysis made on 3 July 2019).

"On July 2, the Reserve Bank of Australia (RBA) cuts rates for the second time in 4 weeks. The first time had been on June 4. The AUD situation is very interesting; I will analyse the currency pair AUDUSD to try and describe a future scenario. Below you can see the daily chart (Figure 76).

Figure 76 - AUDUSD daily chart (TradingView.com)

The two blue lines highlight the two Australian interest rate cuts, while the two black lines put in evidence as support/resistance area (0.70250/0.70500).

The current price might be an excellent level to sell AUDUSD, but there is an aspect to take into account, that is the ideal moment for the gold price which has reached $ 1,440 for the second time (double top?).

The Australian economy is "very sensitive" to gold, so a continuation of the appreciation of the yellow metal could push speculators to buy the Australian dollar.

Thus, you cannot exclude a break of AUDUSD of the resistance because, in the short term, the currencies follow the speculation. But for sure, this would represent (with the right market entry) an excellent opportunity to sell the currency pair (excess of price).

My strategy is the following: I start to sell AUDUSD, using only a part of the position, in the area 0.70250 which is what I call the "spy order" Usually, I use for the spy order 1/4 of the whole position (never more than 1/3).

If the price rebounds on the resistance and then falls, even if it does with a small position, I am nonetheless in the trade. In case AUDUSD breaks the resistance, I have 3/4 of the position to use for selling the currency pair at a better level, with a lower risk."

If the first decision by the Reserve Bank of Australia to cut interest rates was already priced into the market, the second was less obvious, at least after such a short time.

In addition, the currency pair has reached a zone of technical resistance, even though less strong than the one seen on the EURCHF chart. However, the situation was not as strongly on my side as in the previous example.

Shortly after, the United States decided to cut interest rates by 25 basis points and without the crystal ball, I did not know how much this would have an effect (although all analysts foresaw it) on AUDUSD.

If Fed Chairman Powell, in the speech following the communication of the decision taken, had hinted that there would be further rate cuts during the year, the AUDUSD would have jumped well beyond the resistance zone. Hence, the decision to enter only with the spy order, and to wait for the FOMC meeting before making further decisions.

Below, you can see the AUDUSD daily chart a month later (Figure 77).

After a new test of the resistance area (AUDUSD succeeded to break higher), the currency pair began a sharp decline. In this case, I had only opened the spy order, but I could not regret my decision as I know I acted correctly and according to my trading plan.

There was a chance that the AUDUSD could continue to rise for a while (speculation, FOMC meeting…), and I did not want to be in trouble if this scenario materialised.

Figure 77 - AUDUSD daily chart (TradingView.com)

This trade was published on my TradingView account which you can read on https://www.tradingview.com/chart/AUDUSD/OqdiR5Rp-AUD-RBA-cuts-rates-twice-in-4-weeks.

The third and final example concerns EURUSD (analysis made on 1 February 2021).

I start at the end: the FOMC meeting last Wednesday (27 January). Some aspects caught my attention. There is a "weakness concentrated in the sectors of the economy most adversely affected by the resurgence of the virus and by greater social distancing. Household spending on services remains low, especially in sectors that typically require people to gather closely, including travel and hospitality."

However, "the housing sector has more than fully recovered from the downturn, supported in part by low mortgage interest rates. Business investment and manufacturing production have also picked up." The Fed introduces the topic of vaccines by pointing out that "the path of the economy continues to depend significantly on the course of the virus." Significantly, however, a temporal reference to the effects of Covid has disappeared – the disease will continue to affect the economy, employment and inflation "in the short term", the December statement explained, an indication that disappeared in the official January note. The reference to the "medium-term" about the risks created by the virus also disappeared – they are

152

in fact "short-term," Powell said.

At the ECB meeting 6 days earlier, Christine Lagarde points out that "the renewed surge in coronavirus (COVID-19) infections and the restrictive and prolonged containment measures imposed in many euro area countries are disrupting economic activity." By adding that "output is likely to have contracted in the fourth quarter of 2020 and the intensification of the pandemic poses some downside risks to the short-term economic outlook."

At this point, I compared some of the main macroeconomic data of the two economies. For easier and quicker analysis, I constructed the graphs by subtracting the US data from the Eurozone data. In this way, if the graph of a data goes up, except for the Unemployment rate where the opposite is true, it means that the Eurozone has appreciated relative to the US. If the graph goes down, then the US has appreciated more than the Eurozone.

GDP q/q EUROZONE - USA

Figure 78 - GDP graph Eurozone-USA

Unemployment rate EUROZONE - USA

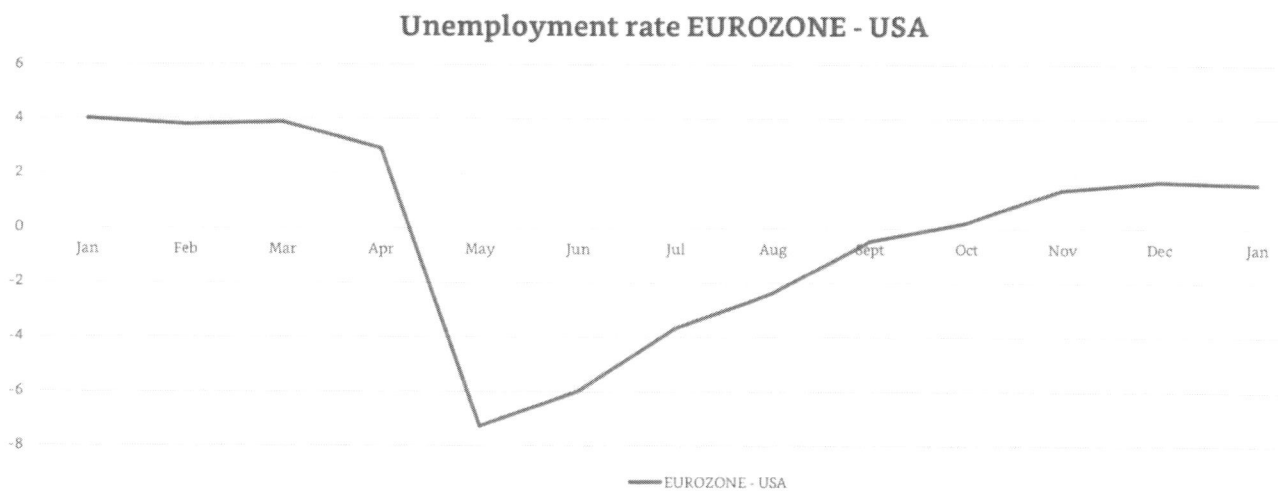

Figure 79 - Unemployment rate graph Eurozone-USA

Above, you can see the graphs of GDP and unemployment rate (Figures 78 and 79); below the graphs of manufacturing PMI and retail sales (Figures 80 and 81), which you have already seen in Chapter 17.

Manufacturing PMI EUROZONE - USA

Figure 80 - Manufacturing PMI graph Eurozone-USA

Retail Sales EUROZONE - USA

Figure 81 - Retail Sales graph Eurozone-USA

In three out of four data, one year later (January 2020-January 2021), the US economy has improved compared to the Eurozone. Only regarding the unemployment rate, twelve months later, did the Eurozone appreciate over the US. Particularly, what emerges from the graphs above is that in the second half of 2020, the US economy appreciated over the eurozone economy. A clarification: the January Eurozone GDP data is the expected one, as it will come out in a few days.

Now, let's look at the chart of EURUSD, to see if the trend has respected the analysis made above (Figure 82).

Figure 82 - EURUSD daily chart (TradingView)

The EURUSD trend is bullish since mid-May, from time to time interspersed with more or less long phases of sideways movements. This is particularly the case since the end of October and does not agree with the analysis of macroeconomic data.

There are no other distinct aspects. The two central banks are continuing their monetary stimulus by injecting liquidity and keeping interest rates steady at current levels for many more months.

At the end of the analysis, it can be argued that the EURUSD exchange rate level is incorrect, it should be lower. The first important levels for EURUSD are 1.21600 (upwards) and 1.18300 (downwards). If conditions and data do not change, my medium to long-term target is in the 1.13000/1.13500 area" (analysis which you can read on my website at https://tradingwithdavid.com/en/eur-usd-fundamental-analysis/.

On 16 November, after nine and a half months, EURUSD reached this area. This example expresses well what the true essence of trading is, and which you will see further explained in the next chapter.

As you have seen, having the odds on your side allows you to work serenely and profitably. Organising everything, with a proper trading plan, will enable you to proceed with your business activity peacefully.

THE ESSENCE OF TRADING

CHAPTER 31

~

In this chapter, I outline how I think and show you my way of working with Forex, starting with the choice of the currency pair, passing through all aspects of the operation (position size, maximum loss, etc.), until the analysis of the currency pair and the strategy to be adopted (entry-level, stop-loss and target). The analysis you will see was made in the middle of April 2021.

Looking at the table of currency pairs I follow, the one that caught my eye was NZDUSD. The price is at a level that is not sustainable in the long run for the New Zealand economy. In the last few years, the area 0.72300/0.72800 has been a very important level for NZDUSD and above that, the currency pair would be in an area of excess price (actually, already above 0.70000 NZDUSD is where excess price has formed).

The operation that I am going to open has a range of the medium-long period, if you are not able to hold an open position for several months, do not replicate it.

Let us proceed. The first thing I decide in each of my operations is how much I am willing to lose. My maximum loss is not equal for all the operations, with some more "particular" I have a smaller propensity to the risk. An example is precisely this operation.

Although NZDUSD belongs to the currency pairs so-called "Majors" the New Zealand dollar is very similar to an "Exotic" currency, therefore with less volume and consequently more volatile and easily speculated. And besides, I already have other long positions on USD. For these reasons, I have decided that my maximum loss on the whole operation is $ 500 dollars – and based on the stop-loss, I will decide the position size to open.

I now analyse NZDUSD trying to understand how it might move in the coming weeks and establish the type of trade and the entry level. In Figure 83, you can see the daily chart with the NZDUSD sensitive levels highlighted.

Figure 83 - NZDUSD daily chart (TradingView.com)

New Zealand's economy had less impact from Covid-19 pandemic than other countries, and this allowed its economy to be less affected. This led to a strong rise in its currency to the 0.75000 area against the US dollar. New Zealand, however, has a strongly export-based economy and with a strong currency, it is not sustainable in the long run.

The New Zealand dollar also strengthened, as many expected the central bank to intervene with a rate hike, "*the Committee agreed that the risks to the economic outlook remain balanced – conditional on ongoing stimulatory fiscal and monetary policies. The Committee agreed that, in line with its least regrets framework, it would not remove monetary stimulus until it had confidence that it is sustainably achieving the consumer price inflation and employment objectives. Given that uncertainty remains elevated, gaining this confidence is expected to take considerable time and patience.*"

However, this is currently unlikely, at least in the short term. Also, because in recent months the New Zealand economy has slowed down, "*Economic activity in New Zealand slowed over the summer months following the earlier rebound in domestic activity. December quarter GDP was weaker than expected and more recent indicators suggest that momentum has reduced. Some members noted that supply chain disruptions could potentially constrain domestic activity in the near term. In addition, business credit growth and investment remain subdued.*"

As for the US, the focus in recent weeks has been on inflation following the entry into force of Biden's economic stimulus plan, "*with inflation running persistently below this longer-run goal (2%), the Committee will aim to achieve inflation moderately above 2 per cent for some time so that inflation averages 2 per cent over time and longer-term inflation expectations remain well-anchored at 2 per cent."*

In March, "Summary of Economic Projections," the PCE inflation forecast for 2021 rose to 2.4% from 1.8% in December, and the Core PCE inflation forecast rose to 2.2% from 1.8% in December. Inflation is forecast at 2.0% in 2022 and 2.1% in 2023 for both. In the same document, you can see (you can find it on the Federal Reserve's website) that in March compared to December the GDP forecast was raised (to 6.5% in 2021 from 4.2% in December) and the unemployment rate lowered (to 4.5% in 2021 from 5.0% in December).

Macroeconomic analysis shows what has already emerged above with New Zealand's data deteriorating in recent months while US data is improving almost steadily. If the vaccination continues apace, the US economy will recover quickly, as the UK economy is doing in Europe.

Once the analysis is complete, how do I intend to proceed? I do not want to open the operation at once. The move is certain, and I would not be surprised to see NZDUSD go up even 300 pips. So, I decided to open a spy order at 0.72400 to see how the currency pair will react to that level.

I will place the primary order, which is larger in size as it is closer to the stop-loss, at 0.73700. For both orders, spy order and primary order, I destine the same maximum loss, which I had decided to be $ 500, so my maximum loss for the two types of orders is $ 250 each. Now with the Value-at-Risk, I calculate the stop-loss and from that, I calculate the size of the two orders. (Refer to page 162 for calculation of each step).

For clarity, I use CVaR to calculate the stop-loss and the calculation gives me a stop-loss of 0.75200. I now calculate the two position sizes.

Ultimately, I will open a short position of $ 9,000 at 0.72400 (spy order) and a short position of $ 17,000 at 0.73700 (primary order), with a stop-loss at 0.75200. As for the target, I always like to see how the currency pair move to assess where to take profit. On 24 January 2022 NZDUSD reached my target in the 0.66400/0.66800 area.

This, somewhat summarises, how I work trading Forex, how I analyse a currency pair and how I organise the whole operation. Back to our question in Chapter 1, what is the essence of Forex?

If you want to earn money with Forex, if you want to make trading a profession in general, you need to be able to analyse the market clearly and accurately. You need to have the exact situation of the currency pair and understand if it has a correct value or if it should be higher or lower. This is the first step you need to take, everything else comes later. If you are not able to understand what level a currency pair is at, what will you do? Will you go long? Short? With what criteria, and on what basis? you need to know your market probabilities and estimate them with complete information to avoid trading mishaps.

Only once you know how to make a clear analysis and think for yourself, you will know what steps you should take, and if the conditions were based upon do not change in the meantime, you will see the currency pair arrive at the target you set. With NZDUSD, the conditions changed a bit over the next few months and, as a result, my analysis changed as well.

The essence of Forex is to gather information and build you thesis correctly – to review your analyse of a currency pair because only in this way you will become a better trader and be an expert in forex. Have a strong picture of the situation and you will know how that currency pair will move in the following weeks/months. Then, the variables are many and it happens that the initial conditions change over time.

To me it has happened many times, not only with NZDUSD, where I re-reviewed my analysis but because the reasoning that had carried me to that conclusion, was not valid anymore. It is part of trading. No one will ever close all trades in profit and above all, no one knows what the future decisions of a central bank will be. They may be in line with your analysis, or they may be surprising and contrary.

Nobody can teach you how to trade, at most they can explain how they trade, as people, we are different, everyone has their own ideas, characteristics, feelings and decisions... Everyone must trade in the way in which it is more congenial to her/him and not follow someone else's model because it would end up finding itself in difficulty. Trading is about preparation and mental endurance and if you aspire to be a professional trader you must be diligent and organise your trading roadmap.

In this book I have not explained how you should trade, but I have showed you how I think and trade - more importantly, how you should correctly analyse a currency pair and how to understand the Forex microstructure of a currency pair through its macroeconomic sphere.

YOUR NEW WAY OF WORKING

CHAPTER 32

~

This journey into currencies between macroeconomics and central banking has come to an end. Before the final comments, in this chapter I will make a practical summary, analysing EURGBP and taking into account all the aspects seen in this book. So that you can see entirely the concepts explained in the various chapters applied to the analysis of a currency pair.

First, in my trading plan I decide how much to lose in case the trade does not go as analysed. This is a personal choice, you must decide on a figure that does not create any problem, neither to your account, nor psychologically from fear, stress, agitation, etc. I do not always decide on the same amount for all currency pairs, it varies depending on the type of currencies used. Personally, I am not willing to lose more than €500 in trades with the British pound and this is the amount I will risk with EURGBP.

At the end of the analysis (on 7 February 2022), based on the entry price (decided using subjective probability) and the stop-loss (calculated using Value-at-Risk), I calculate the position to open. Now, I proceed with the analysis of EURGBP and I do it starting with the central banks.

Below is a summarised points of what emerged from the last Bank of England meeting on 3 February 2022.

- Should not assume rates are on a long march upward.
- We have not raised rates because the economy is roaring away, this is not a standard demand driven rise in the Bank rate.
- We are facing a squeeze on real income this year.
- Would not be surprising if we see a further rate hike, but please do not get carried away.
- Bailey significantly reduced his economic forecasts, saying that UK economic growth would soon "slow to a reduced rate" of around just 1 per cent a year.

There is therefore a possibility that the BoE could start cutting interest rates again in 2023 when it is faced with low economic growth.

The UK is faced with high inflation (forecast by the BoE at 7.25% in April) combined with a weak economy confirming stagflation. In fact, the increase had no effect with the pound retracing on Friday 4 February, losing all the gains of the previous day.

What was striking, was not the 25-basis points rate hike to 0.50% that was widely expected, but the split vote on a larger hike, with 4 members (out of 9) voting in favour of a 50 basis points increase.

The BoE suggests that further hikes may be needed, so money markets are now looking at a possible increase of another 25 basis points at each of the next four meetings. While the decision itself was "hawkish", Governor Bailey hinted at a "dovish" side, in which the message seemed to be hikes now but will stop and reassess.

Below, is what emerged from the European Central Bank meeting, also on 3rd of Feb 2022.

ECB President Lagarde held her more hawkish than expected press conference admitting that Eurozone inflation had peaked at 5.1%, which surprised and caused great concern in the Governing Council.

Although the ECB has left policy unchanged, Lagarde's words have been widely interpreted as a signal of a likely move to tighten monetary policy as early as March, with Lagarde refusing to rule out tightening of monetary policy in 2022.

Markets now expect the deposit rate to rise from -0.5% to -0.1% by December.

Ultimately, Christine Lagarde in her press conference opened the door to a speeding up of asset purchase reductions and a rate hike this year. This pushed the euro strongly up against all other currencies.

That is what the two meetings said. Now, I turn to macroeconomic data, especially, one of them, inflation, which is a reason of concern for the BoE and the ECB.

The annual inflation rate in the euro area rose to a new record high of 5.1% in January from 5% in December 2021, while markets had expected it to slow to 4.4%. Energy continued to record the largest price increase by 28.6%, followed by food, alcohol and tobacco. Core inflation, however, which excludes energy, food, alcohol and tobacco prices, decreased compared to December and November to 2.3%.

The inflation rate remains well above the ECB's target of 2%. Note, one hand an energy crisis in Europe that has sent the cost of natural gas, coal and electricity soaring and on the other hand, improving demand and weak supply related to the pandemic continuing to push commodity prices higher.

The UK annual inflation rate increased to 5.4% in December 2021 from 5.1% in November and above market forecasts of 5.2%. This is the highest reading since March 1992.

The largest contributors to the increase came from the cost of food and non-alcoholic drinks (4.2%), restaurants and hotels (6%), furniture and household goods (7.3%) and clothing and footwear (4.2%).

What can be seen is that the two inflations, Eurozone, and UK, are generated differently. While in the Eurozone it is the energy sector that mainly contributes to the inflation growth, however, in the UK the increase is more homogeneous, spread over several industries.

This can be clearly seen by comparing the Core CPI data on a graph (Figure 84).

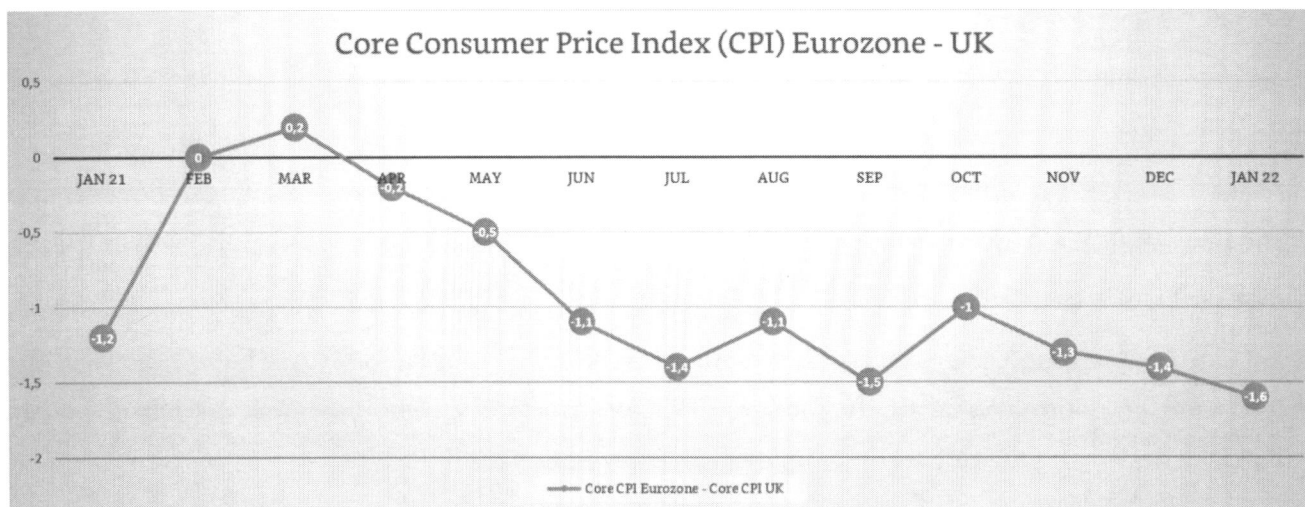

Figure 84 - Core CPI Eurozone-UK

You can visually see how the graph drops as evidence of the above. Data coming out in February should further increase this difference (but we will see that next week).

Here, we have the Eurozone showing more strength in growing its economy and at a faster pace than the UK. Although at the macroeconomic level in the analysis I have not only looked at the inflation figure, but I have also nevertheless analysed the main macroeconomic data and report the conclusions.

Eurozone job prospects are healthier than the UK despite the higher number of unemployed in the EU at 7% compared to the UK at 4.1% (it should not be forgotten that the Eurozone's unemployment rate is the lowest it has been since the introduction of the euro). The UK is still suffering from workers shortages and supply disruption that are also part of labour market due to leaving the EU which prompted to the mass exodus of European workers who occupied these jobs.

Thus far, the analysis is pro-Euro. But there are a couple of cons that left me perplexed. The BoE's repeated interest rate hikes, which, even though I believe they will be detrimental to the British economy in the long term, in the short term could lead institutional investors to prefer the pound rather than the euro for the sake of a better yield (carry trade). This, at least in the short term, would lead to a fall in the EURGBP.

The carry trade is back in vogue in the second half of 2021 pushed by low volatility, rising inflation, and commodities in addition to more austerity from many central banks.

Another possible problem for the Euro is the winds of war in Ukraine. If Russia were to invade Ukraine, the Euro would certainly be the currency among the "Majors" that would be most affected, with a consequent devaluation against the other main currencies.

With confidence, I concluded the Eurozone economy is in better shape than the UK economy, but there are situations that, at least in the short-term, may favour the purchase of Pounds against the Euros.

At this point, I take the chart where I have highlighted the first price sensitive areas. You can see it in Figure 85. For the less experienced I recommend Volume Profile. If you put it on the chart, you can easily see that the levels I have highlighted almost always correspond to the Point of Control (PoC), Value Area High (VAH), Value Area Low (VAL) and High Volume Nodes (HVN).

Figure 85 - EURGBP chart (TradingView)

The first three levels to monitor below the current price of EURGBP are 0.84200/0.83900 area, 0.83500 area and 0.83100/0.82800 area (although the latter is not highlighted in the Chart above). Mind you, there is no guarantee that the currency pair could not fall further. As analysed above, there are a couple of factors that could persuade institutional investors to sell Euros and buy Pounds.

I remain convinced, at least for the moment, that in the medium to long term the Euro will appreciate against the Pound with first targets 0.85100, 0.85950/0.86300 area and final target 0.92000.

So, the strategy I will adopt is as follows. I will place an order to buy EURGBP for 1/3 of my position at 0.83900 (spy order) and afterwards I will evaluate the behaviour of the currency pair. If EURGBP goes up, I can always open the remaining 2/3 of the position (primary order) later (the final target is very distant and still allows me, if reached, to get a very good gain).

If, instead, EURGBP still had to go down, I am inclined to open the primary order in area of 0.82500/0.82800.

As per Chapter 28 you have all the information to proceed with risk management. I will just tell you that the VaR (95%) at one-week is 1.92% while the CVar (95%) is 2.67%. I always use the CVaR (95%), and this means that the stop loss of both the spy order and the primary order will be at 0.81650

Now, the last aspect to be determined is the size of the position. I decided at the beginning of the analysis that my maximum loss for this trade will be € 500. For the spy order at most I want to lose € 150, so with all the data at my disposal, I now calculate the position size by applying the formula already seen in Chapter 27 slightly modified.

[(1,000 * max loss) / pips of stop] / value of 1 pip

So:

<u>Size spy-order</u> = [(1,000 * € 150) / 215] / 0,11987 = € 5,800

While for the primary order (entry at 0.82800):

<u>Size primary order</u> = [(1,000 * € 350) / 115] / 0,11987 = € 25,400

The proportion is not the usual one. Normally, the size of the spy order is 1/3 - 1/4 of the whole position, in this case it is 1/5 but the reason is that I usually split my maximum loss in two (in this case it should have been € 250 for both orders). In view of the two "cons," I have limited the loss of the spy order to only € 150.

<u>Briefly summarising</u>, analysis of the central banks' monetary policy and the economies of the two countries through macroeconomic data shows the Eurozone growing more than the UK and at a faster pace. Inflation is much higher in the UK, and this has led the

BoE to raise rates twice already in 2022 (and further increases are very likely).

Unemployment in the Eurozone is at its lowest level since the introduction of the Euro, the UK is facing a shortage of workers and the disruption of supply, of which the labour market is also a part, due to the exit from the EU which has prompted mass exodus of European workers who were in those jobs.

We saw the main issues the *in favour* of Euro and the *against* the Pound, now let's examine the situations *in favour* of Pound and *against* the Euro.

A more austere monetary policy (and not only) has brought the carry trade back into vogue and with interest rates at zero in the Eurozone and the Bank of England's planned increases this year, but there is also a serious chance that institutional investors will be increasingly tempted to sell Euros and buy Pounds as the yield differential increases. On top of that, the winds of war in Ukraine, with Russia poised to invade the country, are not helping the Euro, which would be the currency (among the Majors) to be most affected if this were to take place.

This is the situation as of 7 February 2022. With an analysis made by putting into practice everything explained in this book (maybe in a different order but nothing changes) I have the correct and precise situation regarding EURGBP. I have chosen the strategy, the entry level and targets, the stop loss and the position size.

And that's how you should work, like a professional stacking the odds on your side. You will not close every trade on target or in profit, as situations evolve, the price action change and so do your analyses and the trends of currency pairs. But you will always know what is going on, whether a currency pair is at a correct level or not, you will be able to make consistent gains over time.

In this book I have explained what Forex is, something very different from what most traders think, using indicators and oscillators to decide what to buy and sell. The forces that move currencies are quite different and if you ignore them, you are doomed to fail. I have tried as much as possible to share part of my experience with you. I hope I have succeeded.

KNOWING THE MARKET WELL

CHAPTER 33

~

And finally, knowing the market you are working with well. This "skill" is acquired with time and experience; understand how a market behaves, its reactions to certain news or data, and its typical movements so that you can exploit them to your advantage. This applies to all assets, not just Forex.

Successful traders understand their market very well and have a deep knowledge of the products they trade not only where the most significant price levels are (as you have seen with subjective probability), but how these currency pairs move and their behaviour. That is why I advise against using all currency pairs in your trading, but to concentrate on only a part of them, those you know best.

Trading is a competitive game. You can't have an edge if you don't have a full understanding of the currency pairs you choose to trade. I only work with 15 currency pairs, about half of all possible combinations (28) of the "Majors" currencies. I do not use the "Exotic" currencies, which are too volatile. For example, I only trade the New Zealand dollar against the US dollar, the Australian dollar and the Japanese yen, and the Canadian dollar only against the US dollar.

This is important, and crucially fundamental I would say, to better manage your trades and not to get crushed by the market at certain junctures. But also, to take advantage, even within an existing trade, by taking momentary contrary movements (countertrend), thus increasing your profit.

Let me show you exactly what I mean with an example. In reference to the analysis made in the previous chapter of EURGBP. To summarise, the analysis gave me a stronger Euro than the Pound and therefore a bullish EURGBP in the following weeks/months, with the first target at 0.85100 and the next in the 0.85950/0.86300 area.

And that's what I did, I entered long on EURGBP. However, I did not leave the trade at the mercy of the continuous ups and downs because of data and speculation but tried to exploit a characteristic the currency pair possesses (or at least has shown to possess so far). The strong retracement that EURGBP makes once a target is reached.

In Figure 86 you can see the daily chart.

Figure 86 - EURGBP daily chart (TradingView)

Highlighted are the two movements of the currency pair once the first and second targets were reached. Also previously, on three occasions EURGBP reached the 0.85950/0.86300 area and then fell strongly. This allowed me to momentarily close the long and open short positions.

Of course, this is not an automatic movement, which happens all the time and will not necessarily continue forever. Much depends on the EURGBP situation once a target has been reached. If the odds are for a continuation of the uptrend, then you are unlikely to see the movement described above. So, as always, you have to analyse the currency pair 360 degrees and assess every aspect and watch its behavioural bias.

Become an expert in your market microstructure so you make more money trading both for those like me who prefer medium-term trading and for those who open short-term trading. Exploit those recurring movements of a currency pair by opening appropriate positions.

This is what automated traders do. They look for biases, i.e., trends that repeat themselves over time, with which to trade. When we talk about bias we are always dealing with time, a bias can be related, for example, to certain times of the day or days of the week.

Let me paraphrase this by saying that I do not trade automatically, not because I do not think it is good but because it is less suited to my characteristics. However, I know traders who make excellent gains from this type of trading, one of them being Andrea Unger. His trading systems have enabled him to become a four-time world trading champion.

To give an example of bias, I have a friend who makes money by trading the pound with different trading systems both intraday and in the short term. I remember him telling me that he buys the GBPUSD and GBPJPY currency pairs 5 days before the end of the month and then closes the trade on the last day of the month. He then sells the same pairs on the first day of the month and buys them back on the 10th of the same month. That's what I mean by deep knowledge of the product you trade by knowing its microstructure.

At the intraday level, he sells the two pairs on both Mondays and Fridays at 8 a.m. (GMT +1) and buys them (closing the trade) at 1 p.m. (GMT +1). And other operations which I do not remember exactly. Please do not use them for trading as my friend adds filters that I do not know of to improve the equity line. Maybe take them as a basis for developing your own strategies.

Overall, these trading systems of his are profitable and give him a profit. To simplify it like that, it may sound easy, but behind it, there are many other aspects to take into account.

Now to conclude this chapter and book, an important consideration. I have told you a little about my type of medium-term trading. However, I am not you, we are different beings and what works for me may not work for you and vice versa. So, you could incorporate what you get from the fundamental analysis of a currency pair into your trading.

I know traders who trade in the short/very short-term and only open trades in the direction of what the fundamental analysis has suggested to them. For example, after analysing EURUSD the pair turns out to be at too high a price, and therefore it is very likely that EURUSD will fall in the coming weeks.

These traders will only go short with trades in the short term, trying to take advantage of bullish movements to identify the best levels where they can open their bearish trades. The information I provided in this book should add information to your trading, not radically change it.

What I have explained to you, such as subjective probability (but also volumetric analysis), Value-at-Risk can be used on different time frames, i.e., you can place (initially) the Volume Profile on a weekly chart or on a 1-hour chart. It depends on your type of trading.

One question I get from time to time is, "by reading this book, do I learn how to trade Forex?" Apart from the fact that reading a book is certainly not enough to learn how to trade, however, I would like to explain this concept once again.

<u>Very important</u>! In this book, I have not explained to you how to trade but how to correctly analyse a currency pair, I have shown you how to buy strength and sell weakness. You must then incorporate this information into your trading. Neither I nor anyone else can teach you how to trade because we are all different people. I can teach you how I trade but what works for me may not work for you. So, it is you who should find your own way, and edge, your ideal type of trading that best suits your personality. My methodology and the concept can be applied to all markets, not just Forex.

In conclusion, each currency pair has its own characteristics that require some time to learn its microstructure if you want to be a real expert in your market. Having a solid understanding of the currency pairs you are working on to feel comfortable with them (without, however, being overconfident which can lead to irrational decisions and overtrading).

That's all. In the next chapter, you will read my conclusions and a brief summary of everything you saw in this book.

FINAL COMMENTS

CHAPTER 34

~

Forex is not only a means to an end (make money with currencies) but something bigger that involves your entire portfolio. A macroeconomic reading teaches you the right way to read the market and manage your portfolio. These concepts will not only come in handy in Forex but in all markets.

A correct reading of the market tells you how you are moving in relation to fundamentals and news, it gives you a statistical advantage. I do not mean that you will always achieve your goals, but you have an advantage – you know where you are, and how to react when the narrative change. Be on the lookout for changes and stay abreast of developments that might change how your market behaves.

You categorically buy strength and sell weakness. Let's buy a weak currency against a potentially strong one just to make better use of short-term expectations (as you have seen with the analysis of GBPUSD). That is the basis of the analysis system. You must not invent anything; you recognise the data and assess the situation.

You must not attempt to anticipate the market or try to predict something according to your own personal views – you must always read only the real situation of a currency pair. Patience is the virtue of the trader. You wait for the right time, and you open a trade when there is an excess in price, when the odds of success are on your side, and, therefore, it is easier for you to profit. A premature market entry, although not quite like flipping a coin, nonetheless reduces your odds by a big margin.

You are not a gambler when you open a trade, and therefore you shouldn't try any tricks that would be out of your control. You are an investor, and investors must always put their money in the market when it has a statistical advantage, not when there is a 50/50 chance of success. This is because, if you hope for this percentage, you might as well go and bet on red or blacks at the roulette table. It is in this regard that you must take the extra steps to differentiate yourself.

You cannot trade without uncertainty, even if you are confident in your

170

knowledge of your market's microstructure – but taking these steps gives you a higher probability of success. If there are no valid conditions, you remain outside of the market because by forcing a trade you will find yourself never meeting these conditions in terms of statistics - always respect the market.

Let's keep in mind that it is not an indicator on a Metatrader (or other) platform that moves the markets in the short-term, but emotions. If, for example, you look at panic selling, all the indicators are in the oversold zone, but the market continues to fall. In other words, indicators are lagging and without a proper plan you put your capital at risk. If you want to work with high percentages, you have to work only in certain specific situations such as volatility – these situations often lead to significant changes in your P&L and can turn profitable strategies into dust and the opposite is true.

As I have explained, I like to work on the price excess, because when the price is misaligned with the macroeconomy, I will get an increase in odds of success. Obviously, the certainty is never 100%, but in the long run, this will give me a profit, if I have followed my trading plan to the letter.

The market invites you to enter, especially when you spend a lot of time in front of the monitor, therefore, whether out of boredom or other factors, a trader tends to trade. A real trader, one that regularly gets a profit, is one who enters the market when he wants, at the price he wants and at the right time.

I know that it is not easy because you are emotionally involved, you get carried away by your feelings, and this sometimes brings you to lose a good occasion to trade. However, this is the right way that will give you long-term survival in the markets and the ability to do very well with excellent profits.

As the market fluctuate, and with high emotions, this is when you must watch your behaviour. That is what makes the difference, especially in the long-term.

Therefore, it is often said that, if you can see the situation calmly, you can also manage it effectively. You decide what to do, the market does not force you to do anything. You manage the situation as you planned and become masters of your trade, and not only that, by doing so, you often go in the wake of investment banks, essentially distancing yourself from the mass.

Everything you have seen in this book is not suitable for "all seasons' strategy", because you always evaluate the historical moment in which you are in. In some situations, it is not unusual to see movements, in short to medium term, that are completely illogical.

That is what has been happening in the markets since the end of February 2020 with the "Covid-19" crisis. Everything seems crazy. Any connection with fundamentals but reality evaporates like a mist hit by the sun when markets collide with the general hysteria of traders, or the need to recover heavy losses from Hedge Funds. Everything loses meaning.

So, do not be surprised if you see the S&P 500 index collapse, and USDJPY rise as shown in the Chart in Figure 87, in periods like this, this can also happen. After all, it is not an ordinary financial crisis, but the result of a pandemic.

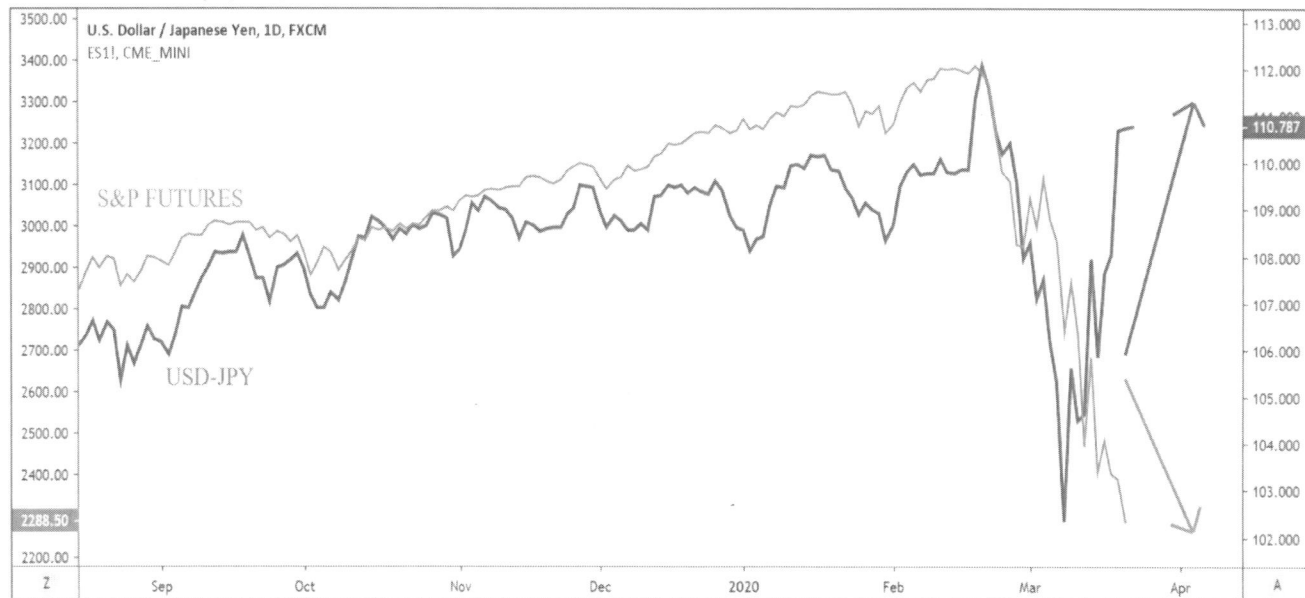

Figure 87 - S&P Futures and USDJPY daily chart (TradingView.com)

My last tip: markets do not give away money. As they say "there's no free lunch in the markets" so, if there are situations that lead you to think so, be very careful.

In conclusion, you have seen the four steps to analyse a currency pair correctly, to understand which of the two currencies, and therefore economies, is the strongest.

You have seen how in the medium to long-term, the Forex market is manipulated by central banks, and how to put yourself in a position to have the odds of success on your side. However, in the short-term is the speculation that moves the market.

For this reason, you must never anticipate market entry. You are better off losing a winning trade than finding yourselves attempting, with difficulty, to manage a losing trade because you opened a position too early. Use the subjective probability to select the best trade entries.

Finally, forget technical analysis. It is not because of this that you will earn in Forex (and in trading in general) consistently. Professional traders do not use technical analysis.

This book is coming to an end; now, all you need to do is practice and gain experience. I understand that what I have tried to explain in the simplest possible way is a series of complicated concepts - at least, to begin with.

Be thoughtful, with time and application you will get used to having a different vision of Forex. You will learn to trade the currencies not by following an indicator anymore, but by considering the fundamental aspects and analysing the two economies that make up a currency pair.

One last thing, at this point, many of you will have commented negatively whenever I mentioned the colours of the charts, "*it is a black and white book, how can I distinguish colours...*" You are absolutely right; the fact is that the same text is also available in the full colour version, and I have not changed anything. However, to help you better understand the colours, I am sending the PDF with all the charts to anyone who requests it by emailing me at info@tradingwithdavid.com or using the form on the "Contact David" page of the site.

I conclude by thanking from the bottom of my heart Hannah for her efforts in proofreading this book into English, she was very kind and professional. You can contact her through her email: hannahhermes@gmail.com.

For any questions my email is info@tradingwithdavid.com. On my website https://tradingwithdavid.com you can find articles, analysis, books, and much more. You find my other books on Amazon: **https://amazon.com/author/davidcarli**.

You can also follow me on:

- **Twitter**: https://twitter.com/tradingwdavid;
- **Instagram**: https://www.instagram.com/tradingwithdavidoriginal/, with operational ideas and discussions of economics and financial markets;
- **YouTube**: https://www.youtube.com/channel/UCHB18Qsl0fm-eBULQEMsVSA;
- **TradingView**: https://www.tradingview.com/u/TradingwDavid.

Do not go yet; one last thing to do.

If you enjoyed this book or found it useful, I would be very grateful if you would post a short review on Amazon. Your support does make a difference, and I read all the reviews personally so I can get your feedback and make this book even better.

Thanks in advance for your support! I really hope that what you have read will help you in your trading.

Happy Trading to you all!

APPENDIX

PIP VALUE

APPENDIX A

~

Below you can see the table with the pip value of the most traded currency pairs.

Currency pair	Pip value (for 1,000 USD)
Aud-Cad	0.07846
Aud-Chf	0.10617
Aud-Jpy	0.07501
Aud-Nzd	0.06458
Aud-Usd	0.1
Cad-Chf	0.10617
Cad-Jpy	0.07501
Chf-Jpy	0.07501
Eur-Aud	0.06431
Eur-Cad	0.07123
Eur-Chf	0.10617
Eur-Gbp	0.12191
Eur-Jpy	0.07501
Eur-Nok	0.01051

Eur-Nzd	0.06458
Eur-Sek	0.00990
Eur-Usd	0.1
Gbp-Aud	0.07123
Gbp-Cad	0.07846
Gbp-Chf	0.10617
Gbp-Jpy	0.07501
Gbp-Nzd	0.06458
Gbp-Usd	0.1
Nzd-Cad	0.07846
Nzd-Chf	0.10617
Nzd-Jpy	0.07501
Nzd-Usd	0.1
Usd-Cad	0.07846
Usd-Chf	0.10617
Usd-Cnh	0.01485
Usd-Jpy	0.07501
Usd-Mxn	0.00501
Usd-Sgd	0.07299
Usd-Zar	0.00616

Table 10 - Pip value (August 12, 2022)

The values in the table above as well as being in US Dollars (and therefore, only available to be used for accounts in that currency) may also undergo, even if mildly, variations over time. In order to have the values in other currencies (for example, EUR, JPY, AUD, etc.) and to update them periodically, you can use the tool available on Myfxbook website (https://www.myfxbook.com/en/forex-calculators/pip-calculator).

WEB RESOURCES

~

Below, summarised, are all the resources you have seen in this book and others as well.

WEBSITE	LINK
Platforms	
TradingView	https://www.tradingview.com
ProRealTime	https://www.prorealtime.com
Metatrader	https://www.metatrader4.com/
Central Banks	
United States	https://www.federalreserve.gov/
Canada	https://www.bankofcanada.ca/
Eurozone	https://www.ecb.europa.eu/home/html/index.en.html
Great Britain	https://www.bankofengland.co.uk/
Switzerland	https://www.snb.ch/en/
Japan	http://www.boj.or.jp/en/index.htm/
Australia	https://www.rba.gov.au/
New Zealand	https://www.rbnz.govt.nz/

China	http://www.pbc.gov.cn/en/3688006/index.html
Reports	
Econ. Projections	federalreserve.gov/monetarypolicy/fomccalendars.htm
Non-Farm Payrolls	https://www.bls.gov/bls/newsrels.htm#OEUS
C.O.T. Report	https://www.cftc.gov
Financial sites	
Barchart	https://www.barchart.com
Finviz	https://www.finviz.com
Investing	https://www.investing.com
Follow me	
Website	https://tradingwithdavid.com
Twitter	https://twitter.com/tradingwdavid
Instagram	https://www.instagram.com/tradingwithdavidoriginal/
YouTube	https://www.youtube.com/channel/UCHB18Qsl0fm-eBULQEMsVSA
TradingView	https://www.tradingview.com/u/TradingwDavid/
Tools	
Pip Calculator	https://www.myfxbook.com/en/forex-calculators/pip-calculator
Resources	
Economic Calendar	https://tradingwithdavid.com/economic-calendar

Table 11 - Web resources

Forex Glossary

~

Aggregate Demand: the sum of government spending, personal consumption expenditures, and business expenditures.

Algorithmic Trading: is a system of executing trades automatically based on advanced mathematical models and formulae that are pre-defined, as opposed to a person manually executing the trade. It is also commonly known as automated trading.

Appreciation: a currency is said to "appreciate" when it strengthens in price in response to market demand.

Arbitrage: the purchase or sale of an instrument and simultaneous taking of an equal and opposite position in a related market, in order to take advantage of small price differentials between markets.

Around: dealer jargon used in quoting when the forward premium/discount is near parity. For example, "two-two around" would translate into 2 points to either side of the present spot.

Ask: the "sell" price, which is sometimes referred to as the offer or Right-Hand Side. The other side of the price is called the "bid" price or the Left-Hand Side.

Asset Allocation: investment practice that divides funds among different markets to achieve diversification for risk management purposes and expected returns consistent with an investor's objectives.

Asset Class: put simply, the classification of an asset. Different types of asset are Foreign Exchange, Equities, Fixed Income and Commodities.

At Best: here you are asking for your trade to be dealt at the best rate available at that time.

Aussie: an abbreviation of 'Australian', referring specifically to the Australian Dollar when used in trading.

Away from the Market: when the current price is higher or lower than your order price it is described as "away from the market."

Back Office: the departments and processes related to the settlement of financial transactions.

Balance of Trade: the value of a country's exports minus its imports.

Bank Rate: the rate at which a central bank lends to members of its banking system.

Bar Charts: standard bar charts are commonly used to convey price activity into an easily readable chart. Usually, four elements make up a bar chart, the Open, High, Low, and Close for the trading session/time period. A price bar can represent any time-frame the user wishes, from 1 minute to 1 month. The total vertical length/height of the bar represents the entire trading range for the period. The top of the bar represents the highest price of the period, and the bottom of the bar represents the lowest price of the period. The Open is represented by a small dash to the left of the bar, and the Close for the session is a small dash to the right of the bar.

Base Currency: in general terms, the base currency is the currency in which an investor or issuer maintains its book of accounts. In the FX markets, the US Dollar is normally considered the 'base' currency for quotes, meaning that quotes are expressed as a unit of $1 per the other currency quoted in the pair. The primary exceptions to this rule are the British Pound, the Euro and the Australian Dollar.

Basis Point: often abbreviated to BPS, is shown as 1/100 of 1%, or 0.0001. That is most commonly applied when quoting interest rates and yield changes. For example, if interest rates are increased from 1.00% to 1.40%, it would be described to have risen by 40 basis points.

Bear: someone of the belief that prices are going to go down.

Bear Market: a market distinguished by declining prices.

Best-Efforts Basis: when a trader executes an order at the price that is next available when there is above average order flow.

Bid: the "buy" price which is sometimes referred to as the bid or Left-Hand Side. The other side of the price is called the "ask" price or the Right-Hand Side.

Bid/Ask Spread: the difference between the bid and offer price, and the most widely used measure of market liquidity.

Big Figure: the first few digits of a Forex rate tend to remain fairly static and these are referred to as the Big Figure. As an example, say for Eur-Usd where the current quote is 1.36782/762, the Big Figure would be 1.36.

Bollinger Bands: are a technical indicator developed by John Bollinger, commonly used by traders to analyse currency price. They are volatility bands based on standard deviation (SD) and placed above and below a moving average. The settings for the Bollinger Bands can be adjusted to suit the particular characteristics of the currency being analysed. The principal rule of the Bollinger Band is that the closer the prices move to the upper band, the more overbought the market, and the closer the prices move to the lower band, the more oversold the market. Technical traders often interpret the tightening of the bands as an early indication that the volatility is about to increase sharply.

Book: in a professional trading environment, a 'book' is the summary of a trader's or desk's total positions.

Break: when prices suddenly move outside a previous range.

Bretton Woods Agreement of 1944: an agreement that established fixed foreign exchange rates for major currencies, provided for central bank intervention in the currency markets, and pegged the price of gold at the US $35 per ounce. The agreement lasted until 1971 when President Nixon overturned the Bretton Woods agreement and established a floating exchange rate for the major currencies.

Broker: an individual or firm that acts as an intermediary, putting together buyers and sellers for a fee or commission. In contrast, a 'dealer' commits capital and takes one side of a position, hoping to earn a spread (profit) by closing out the position in a subsequent trade with another party.

Brokerage: a brokerage or broker is a company that will provide trading in exchange for either fees or commission.

Bull: someone of the belief that prices are going to go up.

Bull Market: a market distinguished by rising prices.

Bundesbank: Germany's Central Bank.

Buying/Selling: in the Forex market currencies are always priced in pairs; therefore, all trades result in the simultaneous buying of one currency and the selling of another. The objective of currency trading is to buy the currency that increases in value relative to the one you sold. If you have bought a currency and the price appreciates in value, then you must sell the currency back in order to lock in the profit.

Buying on Margin: is essentially buying on credit. So, if you execute a trade, only part of the total value of the trade is actually paid for. The part that is paid for is called margin, and the rest is borrowed and will have interest charged.

Buy Stop: this is an order that is used to either close out a short position or start a new long position above market and is usually placed above resistance levels.

Cable: trader jargon referring to the Sterling/US Dollar exchange rate. So-called because the rate was originally transmitted via a transatlantic cable beginning in the mid-1800s.

Candlestick Chart: a chart that indicates the trading range for the day as well as the opening and closing price. If the open price is higher than the close price, the rectangle between the open and close price is shaded. If the close price is higher than the open price, that area of the chart is not shaded.

Central Bank: a government or quasi-governmental organisation that manages a country's monetary policy. For example, the US central bank is the Federal Reserve, and the German central bank is the Bundesbank. others include the ECB, BOE, BOJ.

Chartist: an individual who uses charts and graphs and interprets historical data to find trends and predict future movements. Also referred to as Technical Trader.

Choice Market: a market with no spread. All trades buys and sells occur at that one price.

Clearing: the process of settling a trade.

Collateral: something given to secure a loan or as a guarantee of performance.

Commission: a transaction fee charged by a broker.

Confirmation: a document exchanged by counterparts to a transaction that states the terms of said transaction.

Contagion: the tendency of an economic crisis to spread from one market to another. In 1997, political instability in Indonesia caused high volatility in their domestic currency, the Rupiah. From there, the contagion spread to other Asian emerging currencies, and then to Latin America, and is now referred to as the 'Asian Contagion'.

Contract: the standard unit of trading.

Contract (Unit or Lot): the standard unit of trading on certain exchanges.

Counterparty: one of the participants in a financial transaction.

Country Risk: risk associated with a cross-border transaction, including but not limited to legal and political conditions such as war etc.

Cross Rates: a two-way price made up of one currency quoted against another currency that is not USD. The quote consists of the two individual exchange rates against the USD.

Currency: any form of money issued by a government or central bank and used as legal tender and a basis for trade.

Currency Pair: the two currencies that make up a foreign exchange rate. For example, Eur-Usd (Euro/U.S. Dollar).

Currency Risk: the probability of an adverse change in exchange rates.

Day Trader: speculators who take positions in currency pairs and then liquidate those positions prior to the close of the same trading day.

Day Trading: refers to positions which are opened and closed on the same trading day.

Dealer: an individual who acts as a principal or counterpart to a transaction. Principals take one side of a position, hoping to earn a spread (profit) by closing out the position in a subsequent trade with another party. In contrast, a broker is an individual or firm that acts as an intermediary, putting together buyers and sellers for a fee or commission.

Deficit: a negative balance of trade or payments.

Delivery: an FX trade where both sides make and take actual delivery of the currencies traded.

Depreciation: a fall in the value of a currency due to market forces.

Derivative: a contract that changes in value in relation to the price movements of a related or underlying security, futures or other physical instruments. An Option is the most common derivative instrument.

Devaluation: the deliberate downward adjustment of a currency's price, normally by official announcement.

Discretionary Account: an account where the customer gives someone else permission to make trading decisions for him.

Diversified Carry Basket: a portfolio of carrying trades that are spread out amongst different carry and funding currencies in an attempt to spread the risk and thus limit losses.

Dollar Index (DXY): is an index of the Dollar's value against a basket of six major currencies: EUR, JPY, GBP, CAD, SEK and CHF. The weights of each currency in the index are not representative of US trade, so the DXY is not a particularly good measure of the Dollar's value. It is just a convenient way to take a position on the Dollar in general, instead of versus a specific currency. It was originally created in 1973 by JP Morgan and its components have only been rebalanced once, to take account of the introduction of the Euro.

Dollar Rate: the amount of foreign currency quoted against one US Dollar.

Drawdown: the size of a drop in the value of an account from its peak to its low.

Easing: this term refers to either a small price fall in a currency or when a central bank takes action to try to encourage spending, for example, lowering interest rates.

Economic Indicator: such as GDP, foreign investment, and the trade balance reflect the general health of an economy and are therefore responsible for the underlying shifts in supply and demand for that currency.

End of Day Mark-to-Market: the value of a dealer's book at the end of the day based on the closing market prices. Any P&L is recorded at these rates.

End Of Day Order (EOD): an order to buy or sell at a specified price. This order remains open until the end of the trading day.

Entity Trading Account: a trading account for a company as opposed to an individual with a designated person responsible for any trading decisions.

Escrow Account: a segregated account where customer money is kept separate from a dealer's operating funds.

Euro: since 2002 the Euro has been the currency of the European Monetary Union (EMU). A replacement for the European Currency Unit (ECU). Members of the EMU are Germany, France, Belgium, Luxembourg, Austria, Finland, Ireland, the Netherlands, Italy, Spain and Portugal.

Eurocurrency: a currency that is deposited in a financial institution located outside the currency's country of origin.

EuroDollar: US Dollars deposited in a bank outside the USA.

European Central Bank (ECB): the Central Bank for the new European Monetary Union.

Excess Margin Deposits: funds deposited in a trading account exceeding what is required in margin terms.

Exchange Control: this term refers to strategies used by central banks to prevent depletion of their foreign exchange reserves.

Exchange Rate: what one currency is worth against another. Currencies have a spot rate which refers to trades settled in two business days and a forward rate, which is the spot rate adjusted to show the interest rate differential between the two.

Execution: completing a trade.

Exit: this is essentially closing your position. So, if you are long, you will sell, and if you are short, you will buy.

Exotics: Exotic Currencies are those that are traded infrequently and in very small volumes in comparison to the major currencies. They are called such due to their rarity in the global market. Exotic Currencies are not as widely available for trade through normal brokerage accounts. They carry a contrasting set of characteristics to major currencies. They are, as a rule, less liquid and carry a considerably lower volume than major currencies. As such, they require less influence to cause a major wave. A trade that may carry no influence on a major pair may carry a greater influence on an exotic pair as there is less volume in and out to dilute the trade in that particular market. Trading an exotic currency can be expensive, as the bid-ask spread is usually large, they are potentially hostile and more volatile than major pairs.

Exposure: the net of all long and short positions for a particular currency. Based on the trader's positions for all currencies, his/her exposures can result in either loss or gain.

Fast Market: when prices move particularly quickly, often meaning that trades cannot be executed fast enough.

Federal Deposit Insurance Corporation (FDIC): the regulatory agency responsible for administering bank depository insurance in the US.

Federal Reserve: the central bank of the United States, with responsibility for implementing the country's monetary policy and regulating member banks of the System. The Fed was created in 1913 and is composed of 12 regional Federal Reserve Banks and a national Board of Governors.

Fibonacci Technical Study: the Fibonacci Fans and Bands are three-line guides drawn onto charts. They are derived from the Fibonacci number sequence, discovered by Leonardo Fibonacci. This sequence is written as follows: 1, 1, 2, 3, 5, 8, 13, 21, 34, 55... Infinitely, where the next number is equal to the sum of the two previous. Each number to the next has a ratio of .618, whilst each alternating number has a ratio of .382. Interestingly, these add up to 1, and the halfway point of the two is .50. Therefore, .382, .50, and .618 are the three numbers used for calculating the aforementioned lines, which some traders believe can be used to pinpoint areas of support and resistance.

Fixed Exchange Rate: official rate set by monetary authorities for one or more currencies.

Flat/square: dealer jargon used to describe a position that has been completely reversed, e.g. you bought $500,000 then sold $500,000, thereby creating a neutral (flat) position.

Flexible Exchange Rate: an exchange rate that is fixed, but is re-evaluated frequently.

Floating Exchange Rates: floating exchange rates refer to the value of a currency is decided by supply and demand.

Foreign Exchange: (Forex, FX) is the simultaneous buying of one currency while selling for another. This market of exchange has more buyers and sellers and daily volume than any other in the world. Taking place in the major financial institutions across the globe, the Forex market is open 24-hours a day.

Forward: the pre-specified exchange rate for a foreign exchange contract settling at some agreed future date, based upon the interest rate differential between the two currencies involved.

Forward Contract: a forward contract fixes the exchange rate for future delivery at a date to be agreed by both participants. A deposit (or a minimum margin) is usually required in forwarding transactions. For example, if I want to lock in today's rate to buy $10,000 at 1.5820 Canadian for the next 4 months, I will have the ability to purchase up to $10,000 at this rate.

Forward Points: the pips added to or subtracted from the current exchange rate to calculate a forward price.

Forward Rates (Swaps): a Forward Rate refers to a cash price of 2 currencies interest difference for a fixed term. Forward rates can be calculated easily given the fixed term interest rates of each currency and the current spot rate.

Forward Trading: forward trading is making the opposite trade of a spot trade in a given period of time. Often investors will swap their trades forward for anywhere from a week or two up to several months depending on the time-frame of the investment. Even though a forward trade is on a future date, the position can be closed out at any time. The closing part of the position is then swapped forward to the same future value date.

Fundamental Analysis: focuses on the economic forces of supply and demand that cause price movement. The Fundamentalist studies the causes of market movement, whereas the Technician studies the effects.

Futures Contract: an obligation to exchange a good or instrument at a set price on a future date. The primary difference between a Future and a Forward is that Futures are typically traded over an exchange (Exchange-Traded Contacts – ETC), versus forwards, which are considered Over The Counter (OTC) contracts. An OTC is any contract NOT traded on an exchange.

Gearing: also known as margin trading. A term used in the relationship between actual equity versus controlling equity.

Golden Cross: the point at which two moving averages intersect, which is generally considered to be a good sign that the underlying currency will move in the same direction.

Goldilocks Economy: was a term coined back in the mid-1902 to describe an economy that was not too hot and not too cold. That typically describes an economy that enjoyed steady growth with the nominal rate of inflation.

Good 'til Cancelled (GTC): an order to buy or sell at a specified price. This order remains open until filled or until the client cancels.

Good 'til Date: an order to buy or sell at a specified price that will expire on a specific date. If the order has not been executed by the expiry date, the order will be cancelled.

Hard Currency: a currency that investors have confidence in. Examples could be the US Dollar or the Euro.

Head and Shoulders: a price trend pattern which has three peaks, the middle one higher than the surrounding two forming what looks to be a head with two shoulders on either side. This pattern is seen as an indicator of a trend reversal. The left shoulder is typically formed at the end of an extensive move where volume is noticeably high. Once the left shoulder is formed, the market reacts and price slides. When price recovers, it rallies up to form a peak at the head greater than the peak of the left shoulder. Price then reacts down again to form a second trough. The right shoulder is formed when prices move up again, but to a level lower than the peak of the head and then fall to below the peak of the left shoulder at the very least. A neckline is formed by connecting the lowest points of the two troughs. The slope of this line can either be up or down depending on the depth of each trough, respectively. When the slope is down a more reliable signal.

Hedging: a hedging transaction is a purchase or sale of a financial product, having as its purpose the elimination of loss arising from price fluctuations. With regards to currency transactions, it would protect one against fluctuations in the foreign exchange rate. (see Forward Contract).

High/Low: refers to the daily traded high and low price.

IFEMA: acronym for International Foreign Exchange Master Agreement.

Indicative Quote: a price quoted by a market maker as an indicator rather than a definite price.

Inflation: an economic condition whereby prices for consumer goods rise, eroding purchasing power.

Initial Margin: the initial deposit of collateral required to enter into a position as a guarantee of future performance.

Interbank Rates: the Foreign Exchange rates at which large international banks quote other large international banks.

Intraday Trading: positions that are opened and closed within the same trading day.

Key Currency: when smaller economies align their exchange rate to that of a more dominant currency, this latter currency is known as a key currency. For example, the Euro or US Dollar are both common key currencies.

Kiwi: trader's term for the New Zealand Dollar.

Leading Indicators: statistics that are considered to predict future economic activity.

Leading Side: if spot is going higher, the leading side of the price is the offer because it gets to the higher point first. If spot is going lower, the bid gets there first and is the leading side.

Left-Hand Side: the "buy" price which is sometimes referred to as the bid or Left-Hand Side. The other side of the price is called the "ask" price or the Right-Hand Side.

Leverage: by definition, leverage is "the exertion of force by means of a lever or an object used in the manner of a lever." In financial terms, the 'lever' can mean to reinvest debt in an effort to earn a greater return than the cost of interest. When a firm uses a considerable proportion of debt to finance its investments, it is considered highly leveraged. In the world of Forex, this leaver is borrowed capital or margin. The greater the value of leverage, the greater the ratio of margin to the maximum position size. With a deposit of $ 5000 and a leverage of 50, a trader could enter a position with a face value of $ 250,000. Leveraging allows you to profit quickly, but lose money just as fast. See also Margin.

Liability: the obligation to deliver the currency as part of a spot transaction. In speculative Forex trading, the currency is not delivered. All profits and losses are added to or subtracted from margin deposits.

LIBOR: the London Inter-Bank Offered Rate. Banks use LIBOR when borrowing from another bank.

Limit order: an order with restrictions on the maximum price to be paid or the minimum price to be received. As an example, if the current price of Usd-Jpy is 102.00/05, then a limit order to buy USD would be at a price below 102. (i.e. 101.50).

Limit Price: the specified price as part of a limit order.

Line Charts: the Line Chart connects single prices for a selected time period.

Liquid: the term used where there are large supply and demand for a particular asset, which usually means that spreads are tight and availability is plentiful. The opposite of this is illiquid markets, whereby there is less availability and subsequently spreads tend to be wider.

Liquidation: the closing of an existing position through the execution of an offsetting transaction.

Liquidity: the ability of a market to accept large transaction with minimal to no impact on price stability.

Long position: a position that appreciates in value if market prices increase. When one buys a currency, their position is long.

Lots: one standard lot in the FX market is 100,000 units of the base currency. That would mean €100,000 of Eur-Usd, $100,000 of Usd-Jpy, etc. There are also **mini-lots** of 10,000 units and **micro-lots** of 1,000 units. A micro-lot is usually the smallest available unit for trading.

Majors: refers to the major currencies that are traded: USD, EUR, GBP, CHF, AUD, CAD, NZD, and JPY. Also known as Principals.

Managed Float: a "deposit" that is made as collateral towards the total amount of trade.

Margin: is a percentage of the total value of a transaction. It is the collateral payment made by a trader to secure leverage. For example, if a trader places a £ 1000 margin for the control of £ 10,000, their leverage would be 10:1 as they are now in control of ten times their initial payment. Therefore, in this instance, the margin would be 10%.

Margin Account: an account that lets you trade on credit.

Margin Call: is made when your account is in deficit. To avoid liquidation, positions will need to be either closed or reduced or alternatively, additional funds will need to be added to the account. Note: In a fast-moving market, there may be little time between margin alerts, or there may not be sufficient time to receive the warning. It is very important for individuals to proactively manage the status of their accounts.

Margin Requirement: the minimum collateral that is needed on an account before executing a trade.

Mark-To-Market: the process of re-evaluating all open positions with the current market prices. These new values then determine margin requirements.

Market Maker: someone who "makes a market" or who provides two-way quotes against which they are either willing to buy or sell. Market makers earn their money from the spread on a price – the difference between the bid and offer price.

Market Order: an order for immediate execution at the best available price.

Market Risk: the risk associated with investing in the market. For example, high volatility often translates into high risk. Occasionally, market risk is also known as systematic risk.

Maturity: the date for settlement or expiry of a trade.

Mid: the price halfway between the bid and ask quote offered by dealers. For example, if the bid is 1.4426 and the ask is 1.4430, the mid-price is 1.4428.

Moving Average: method of smoothing out data on price charts so that trends are easier to spot. Average refers to a mathematical average or a statistical mean that is plotted over the original curve.

Narrow Market: also referred to as a thin market, where there is light trading, low liquidity, high volatility and high spreads. That is the polar opposite.

Net Account Value: this is your overall account balance, so all your cash plus or minus any unrealised profit or losses.

Net Position: currency positions that have not yet been offset with opposite positions.

News Trader: an investor who bases his/her decisions on the outcome of a news announcement and its impact on the market.

Non-Farm Payrolls (NFP): this figure is released on the first Friday of every month and represents the total number of paid workers of any business, excluding farm, general government, private household and non-profit organisations that provide assistance to individuals employees in the United States. The NFP report also contains estimates of the averages of the workweek and weekly earnings of all Non-Farm employees.

Offer: the "sell" price, which is sometimes referred to as the ask price or Right-Hand Side. The other side of the price is called the "bid" price or the Left-Hand Side.

Options: these are tradable contracts giving the right, but not obligation, to buy or sell currencies at a future date and a prearranged price. Options are used to hedge against adverse price movements or to speculate against price rises or falls. Trading options is riskier than trading spot currency but offers potentially higher returns.

Order: an instruction to buy or sell a specified amount at a specified rate, which remains valid until the trade is completed or until a time that is stated. The two most common types of orders are limit and Stop-loss orders.

Oscillators: an Oscillator is in effect, the measurement of an object be it physical, graphical or data, that moves back and forth between two given points. The movement is called oscillation, and at all times, this will occur between the two given points. In Forex, Oscillators are Technical Analysis tools that provide buy and sell signals, characterised by a signal that oscillates between overbought and oversold levels. Examples of different Oscillators in Forex would be, The Stochastic, Parabolic SAR, and Relative Strength Index (RSI). Each of these is designed to signal a possible reversal where the price is ready to change direction. Oscillators are also often known as Leading Indicators.

Over The Counter (OTC): refers to trading that is not done over a formal exchange. Traditional Forex is traded over the counter, meaning traders entered into Forex transactions with another counterparty rather than through an exchange.

Overbought: a currency pair is overbought when its price rises much more quickly than usual in response to net buying. Once overbought, the pair is then expected to make a contrarian move, meaning its price is expected to fall.

Overnight: trades that extend past the current trade day into the next.

Oversold: a currency pair is oversold when its price falls much more quickly than usual, declining too far in response to net selling. Once oversold, the pair is then expected to make a contrarian move, meaning its price is expected to rise.

Pip: The word 'pip' is an acronym for 'percentage in point.' The term has historically referred to the smallest incremental movement in price in the currencies trading market. The majority of currency pairs were quoted to four decimal places, so the smallest pip movement was that of the fourth decimal place. For example, if Eur-Usd rose from 1.3975 to 1.3977, it had risen two pips. There were some exceptions. The Japanese Yen (JPY) was priced to just two decimal places so a currency pair with JPY as the quote currency would have a pip equal to 0.01. A move in Usd-Jpy of 128.50 to 128.51 was one pip. In 2005 we were instrumental in introducing an additional decimal point to pricing in the interbank market.

Political Risk: exposure to changes in governmental policy which will have an adverse effect on an investor's position.

Position: the netted total holdings of a given currency.

Premium: in the currency markets, describes the amount by which the forward or futures price exceed the spot price.

Price: the cost of purchasing a second currency in terms of a first currency.

Price Transparency: describes quotes to which every market participant has equal access.

Profit/Loss or "P&L": the actual "realised" gain or loss resulting from trading activities on closed Positions, plus the theoretical "unrealised" gain or loss on open positions that have been Mark-to-Market.

Quantitative Easing: the act of a country's central bank increasing the amount of money in the economy at a time when interest rates are very low as a way of increasing economic growth.

Quote: an indicative market price, normally used for information purposes only.

Rally: a recovery in price after a period of decline.

Range: the difference between the highest and lowest price of a currency pair during a given trading period.

Rate: the price of one currency in terms of another, typically used for dealing purposes.

Re-quotes: occur when you place an "at the market" order and find that your order was filled, or executed, at a different price than what had appeared on the screen at the time you place your order. Sometimes this is unavoidable, as when the market is moving quite quickly, and the price has changed in the few seconds between your pressing the button and the broker executing your trade. But sometimes it is not unavoidable at all; sometimes unscrupulous brokers put attractive prices up on their screens in order to win business, but then execute incoming trades at prices that are more advantageous to them.

Resistance: a term used in technical analysis indicating a specific price level at which analysis concludes people will sell.

Retail FX Market: comprises a wide range of non-institutional traders, from large organisations to individual investors.

Revaluation: an increase in the exchange rate for a currency as a result of central bank intervention. Opposite of Devaluation.

Revaluation Rates: the revaluation rates are the market rates used when a trader runs an end-of-day to establish profit and loss for the day.

Right Hand Side: refers to the Ask or Offer price. That is the price at which traders buy.

Risk: exposure to uncertain change, the variability of returns significantly the likelihood of less-than-expected returns.

Risk Capital: the amount of money that an individual can afford to invest, which, if lost would not affect their lifestyle.

Risk Management: to hedge one's risk they will employ financial analysis and trading techniques.

Roll-Over: the process whereby the settlement of a deal is rolled forward to another value date. The cost of this process is based on the interest rate differential of the two currencies.

Rollover Rate: the daily rollover interest rate is the amount a trader either pays or earns, depending on the established margin and position in the market. To avoid rollovers simply make sure positions are closed at the established end of the market day.

Scalping: is a form of extremely short-term trading. Scalpers frequently trade, going both long and short a currency pair, with the aim of making many small profits on intraday moves. Scalpers often try to profit from the increase in volatility that occurs when major economic indicators are released.

Sell Limit Order: an order to enter a position only at a specified price (the limit) or higher.

Sell Stop: a limit order with a limit placed below the current market price. Once triggered, the limit order becomes a market order.

Selling Short: selling a currency pair that involves being short the base currency and long the quote currency, with the intent of buying the currency pair at a later time when prices are lower in order to make a profit.

Settlement: the process by which a trade is finalised and entered into the books and records of the counterparts to a transaction, normally two business days after the trade.

Short: selling a currency, with the intent of buying it at a later time when prices are lower in order to make a profit.

Short Position: an investment position that benefits from a decline in market price. When one sells a currency, their position is short.

Slippage: occurs when you place an order to be filled at a specified rate, but it is filled at a different rate than you requested. For example, you might be long EUR/USD overnight with a stop-loss order to sell your position if it falls to a certain level, but find when you wake up that the market went through that level and you were stopped out at a worse level than you wanted, thereby losing more money than you had budgeted for.

Spike: when a price moves unexpectedly.

Spot: a currency deposit transaction or the simultaneous purchase and sale of a currency, or vice versa by means of swap for spot value day against the next working day.

Spot Price: the current market price. Settlement of spot transactions usually occurs within two business days.

Spot (Rate): in FX Markets, Spot refers to the cash price without interest factored in.

Spot Trade: when you trade foreign exchange, you are always quoted a spot price 2 business days in advance. That is under normal conditions where there are no bank holidays in the traded currencies countries or is not over a weekend.

Spread: the difference between the bid (buy) and offer (ask, sell) prices; in other words, the spread is the commission that the brokerage house makes on each trade. That can vary widely between currencies and between brokerage firms. For example, Usd-Jpy may bid at 131.40 and ask at 131.45, this five-pip spread defines the trader's cost, which can be recovered with a favourable currency move in the market.

Square: purchase and sales of currencies are in balance, and thus, the trader has no open position.

Sterling: slang for British Pound.

Stop-loss: order type whereby an open position is automatically liquidated at a specific price, often used to minimise exposure to losses if the market moves against an investor's position. As an example, if an investor is long USD at 156.27, they might wish to put in a stop-loss order for 155.49, which would limit losses should the dollar depreciate, possibly below 155.49.

Stop-loss Strategy: a trading strategy that involves setting limit orders at different price levels to avoid incurring further losses.

Stochastic Oscillator: this technical analysis indicator is based on the premise that during an upward trading market, prices tend to close near their highs, and during a downward trading market, prices tend to close near their lows.

Strike Price: the price at which the underlying asset can be bought or sold as specified in an option contract.

Support Levels: a term used in technical analysis indicating a specific price level at which a currency will have the inability to cross below. Recurring failure for the price to move below that point produces a pattern that can usually be shaped by a straight line. It is the opposite of Resistance levels.

Swap: a currency swap is the simultaneous sale and purchase of the same amount of a given currency at a forward exchange rate.

Swap Price: a price adjustment, added to the opening price of the position, for forwarding a Forex trade beyond the original value date. It is a function of the interest rate differential between the two trading currencies and can be in your favour or against you.

Swift: Society of Worldwide Interbank Financial Telecommunications. It is a dedicated computer network that is set up to support fund transfer messages between member banks worldwide.

Swissy: another name for the Swiss Franc.

Take Profit: a limit order that is placed above the market with a long position or below the market with a short position. When the market reaches the limit price, the position is closed thereby locking in a profit.

Technical Analysis: an effort to forecast prices by analysing market action through chart study, volume, trends, moving averages, patterns, formations and many other technical indicators.

Technical Correction: a price adjustment based on technical factors like resistance and support levels, as well as overbought and oversold levels, instead of market sentiment.

Technical Indicators: short-term trends that technical analysts use to predict future price movements of securities and commodities. Also called technicals, technicalities.

Tick: minimum price move.

Ticker: shows a current and recent history of a currency either in the format of a graph or table.

Tomorrow Next (Tom/Next): simultaneous buying and selling of a currency for delivery the following day.

Trade Date: the date on which a position is opened.

Trading: buying or selling of goods and services among countries called commerce. Forex Trading is the trading of Foreign Currencies.

Trailing Side: if spot is going higher the trailing side of the price is the bid if spot is going lower the offer is the trailing side.

Trailing Stop: a trailing stop-loss order is in effect a stop-loss order that follows your trade around and closes it out when the price has moved a certain amount from the highest level since the inception of the trade. Trailing stops are set in terms of the number of pips, not levels.

Transaction Cost: the cost of buying or selling a financial instrument.

Transaction Date: the date on which a trade occurs.

Trend: simply the direction of the market, usually broken down to three categories: major, intermediate and short-term trends. Three directions are also associated.

Trend Line: this is a Technical Analysis indicator, also called or linear regression, which is a statistical tool used to uncover trends. It is calculated by using the "Least Squares" method. There are two ways to use the linear regression line: a. Trade in the direction of the Trend line. b. Construct a parallel trend channel above and below the Trend line to be used as support and resistance levels.

Turnover: the total money value of all executed transactions in a given time period; volume.

Two-Way Price: when both a bid and offer rate is quoted for an FX transaction.

Unconvertible Currency: a currency that cannot be exchanged for another because of foreign exchange regulations.

Undervalued: when a currency is below its purchasing power parity it is considered undervalued.

Unit: a widely used quantity of currency.

Unrealised Profit/Loss (Unrealised P&L): a valuation of the current position and the resultant profit or loss if the position were to be liquidated at that moment. They become realised profits or losses when the position is closed.

Uptick: a new price quote at a price higher than the preceding quote.

Uptick Rule: in the U.S., a regulation whereby a security may not be sold short unless the last trade prior to the short sale was at a price lower than the price at which the short sale is executed.

Us Dollar: the currency of the United States of America.

US Prime Rate: the interest rate at which US banks will lend to their prime corporate customers.

Value Date: the date on which counterparts to a financial transaction agree to settle their respective obligations, i.e., exchanging payments. For spot currency transactions, the value date is normally two business days forward. Also known as the maturity date.

Variable Currency: in Forex, this is the currency that the investor pays with or receives when trading. For example, in Eur-Usd, the variable currency is USD, that is, one unit of EUR is worth a variable amount of USD. When you buy EUR, you pay with USD, and when you sell EUR you receive USD. The other currency (EUR in the example above) is called the base currency.

Variation Margin: funds a broker must request from the client to have the required margin deposited. The term usually refers to additional funds that must be deposited as a result of unfavourable price movements.

Volatility: a measure of price fluctuations. The standard deviation of a price series is commonly used to measure price volatility.

Volatility Index (VIX): shows the market's expectation of 30-day volatility. It is constructed using the implied volatilities of a wide range of S&P 500 index options. The VIX is a widely used measure of market risk and is often referred to as the "investor fear gauge."

Volume: represents the total amount of trading activity in a particular stock, commodity or index for that day. It is the total number of contracts traded during the day.

Weak Dollar/ Strong Dollar: Dollar is said to be weak (relative to a previous time period) against another currency when more Dollars are required to buy one unit of another currency. The Dollar is strong or has gained in strength when fewer Dollars are required to buy one unit of another currency. For example, if $ 1 buys 3 Swiss Franc in 1989, but today $ 1 buys only 1.5 Swiss Franc then the Dollar has weakened against CHF.

Whipsaw: slang for a condition of a highly volatile market where a sharp price movement is quickly followed by a sharp reversal.

Working Day: when the banks in the country of origin for a particular currency are open for business. For currency pairs, this is compounded by the fact that both banks must be open.

Yard: slang for a billion.

YIELD: return on capital investment.

TwD

Made in United States
North Haven, CT
27 December 2022